KENT SHIPWRECKS

ALAN BIGNELL

COUNTRYSIDE BOOKS
NEWBURY, BERKSHIRE

Also by Alan Bignell:

Tales of Old Kent
The Kent Village Book

First Published 1991
© Alan Bignell 1991, 2001

Second Edition 2001

COUNTRYSIDE BOOKS
3 Catherine Road
Newbury, Berkshire

To view our complete range
of books, please visit us
at www.countrysidebooks.co.uk

ISBN 1 85306 719 9

Cover illustration by Jenny Morgan

Produced through MRM Associates Ltd., Reading
Printed by J.W. Arrowsmith Ltd., Bristol

CONTENTS

Introduction

Despite all the advances in ship building techniques and material, all the technological developments that have been introduced to compensate for the human fallibility of ships' crews, and all the ingenuity that has gone into the management of busy shipping lanes, the sea continues to take its toll of ships and the people who sail in them.

Down the centuries, the English Channel has gathered in a copious share of that tragic toll, much of it from the extreme south-east corner, around the coast of Kent.

No-one can tell you how many ships have been wrecked off the Kent coast. Richard Larn, who is reckoned to be the authority on the subject, has published charts which plot the positions of several hundred vessels wrecked along the north, east and south coasts of the county in the last 200 years and almost as many again on the Goodwin Sands alone. But he acknowledges that an additional 900 shipwrecks have been recorded and it is estimated that at least another 500 vessels have been lost without trace in these waters.

Whatever the actual total, it is certainly very considerable because for as long as ships have been sailing past the east coast of England, along the north coast of Kent, round the North Foreland and into the English Channel – and, of course, in the opposite direction as well – ships have also been running aground on the shoals and sandbanks, rocks and beaches of this, perhaps, the most varied and one of the most hazardous coastlines of any in England.

You need only to glance at a chart of the seas around the 180-mile long coastline from the Thames Estuary to Dungeness to understand why so many vessels of all sizes have been wrecked in these waters. The whole seaway is a maze of channels through sandbanks that are continually being sculpted into new shapes by tides and currents that never seem to be quite satisfied with their creations. The Kent coast turns through an almost geometric right angle round the 'parson's nose' of the North Foreland and that alone gives rise to unusually strong and treacherous currents, sudden changes of wind speed and direction, and wayward tidal flows. Add to all this the narrowness of the sea between that coastline and the French coast opposite, and the fact that, for centuries, this has been one of the world's busiest seaways, and the potential for disaster is at once apparent.

Today, collisions are the most common major mishaps at sea. The huge size of the vessels that ply the Channel and the restrictions to their manoeuvrability, together with the often dangerously volatile character of their cargoes, make a collision between two of these monsters a fearful event indeed. Nevertheless, it has become increasingly rare for such events to result in traditional shipwreck and consequential loss of life. Much more often than in the past, collisions leave the two vessels damaged but still afloat and able to reach a friendly dock. There are exceptions, and ships do still, from time to time, sink but the number of wrecks littering the seabed around the Kent coast is not being added to as often now as it once was.

By far the most notorious of the Kent coast hazards is the Goodwin Sands. It is legend, not history, that claims the Sands are all that remain of a once fertile Isle of Lomea, part of the extensive domains of the great Lord Godwin, Earl of Kent and father of that King Harold who lost his eye, his throne and his life in one memorable day in 1066. The story goes that Godwin neglected the sea defences of his island, which was inundated in one great storm and became the almost equally legendary *Shippe*

Swallower of medieval notoriety: one of the most feared navigational hazards in the world.

At low tide, in summer, the Goodwin Sands bathe in the mild balminess of the favoured south-east, firm enough to drive racing cars on them and beguiling enough for the occasional novelty of a game of cricket or golf, or for cycling races.

But at high tide, when winter gales lash the few feet of water that covers them into a foaming frenzy in which few vessels can hope to survive intact for very long, they become a grasping, voracious and insatiable maw into which whole vessels have been known to disappear without trace in a matter of minutes.

The Goodwin Sands have their own special technique for consuming their prey. Patiently, they lie in wait for their allies, wind and tide, to drive their victims firmly into their embrace. There they hold them, tenaciously, while those same allies pound the helpless victims. Then, by allowing a falling tide to scour the sand out from under the bows and stern of the ship, or from amidships, they create a hog's back or else a basin, so that in either case the helpless vessel breaks its back, to be consumed by the soft, sucking sand beneath her two parts.

In certain places and in certain conditions, the whole process can be completed within an hour so that before rescuers can reach the scene, or sometimes even realise there is a ship in distress, little more than a spar of flotsam remains to confirm the tragedy.

Of such a phenomenon as the Goodwin Sands there are, inevitably, many legends and many stories. One man who did as much as any other to clothe legend in a few hard facts was George Goldsmith Carter in his book *The Goodwin Sands*, which was first published in 1953. His personal knowledge of the Sands came from service on the North Goodwin lightship and his opening description of the low tide landscape presented by the Sands is not to be missed by anyone who wants to understand better this unique area of offshore topography.

Another, earlier, writer was George Byng Gattie, whose book *Memorials of the Goodwin Sands* (first published in 1890) contained a full account of the history and some of the many legends of the origins of the Sands.

The Goodwins lie some four to six miles off Deal, a series of sandbanks ten or eleven miles long and about four miles across, separated by channels, all constantly changing shape and positions. At high spring tides, the Sands are covered by about twelve feet of water, but at low water up to seven feet of dry, firm land is exposed. Charts show the Sands looking a bit like a lobster, with a huge claw extending south-west, its tips being the north and south callipers of the Goodwins. The curve of the body of the lobster shape is Trinity Bay. The main body of the Sands tends to drift very slowly south-south-west. They shift and change shape and in 1846 Bunt Head, a bank of sand between the Goodwins and the mainland, vanished altogether.

Near the East Goodwin lightship, the Sands shelve rapidly into deep water. They are completely hidden at high water and are deadly to shipping. This is where most shipwrecks occur. There is a strong current round the North Foreland into the Dover Strait which can push vessels towards the Sands.

The Goodwins were surveyed in 1798 by John Smeaton and in 1817 Trinity House borings decided that the sand was 15 ft deep on a bed of chalk and blue clay. When Admiral Bullock built a safety beacon on the Goodwins in 1840, he reported that at seven and a half feet deep the sand was so dense it broke his boring tool.

One of the channels through the sands is The Downs, partially enclosed to the east by the Goodwins. The Downs have been a traditional refuge for ships in some of the greatest gales history has flung against this coast. The Sands create a natural breakwater and ships sheltering at anchor in The Downs may hope to ride out the storm in comparative safety.

Not all do, of course. In the great storm of November 1703, when an entire fleet of 13 warships under Rear Admiral Basil Beaumont sought shelter in The Downs, a gale that had blown for several days already, increased in strength to a force

8

unparalleled in human memory at that time and blew for eight hours, throughout one night. By morning, not one of the vessels that had been anchored there at nightfall remained. Every one had been totally wrecked on the Sands or driven on to the shore, with appalling loss of life.

In February 1807, another great storm wrecked at least 21 vessels, some of which were claimed by the Goodwin Sands while the rest were driven ashore between Deal and the South Foreland, again with great loss of life.

In November 1836, as many as 250 ships were reported to have been wrenched from their anchorages in The Downs. Many of these, too, were driven on to the Sands, or blown ashore, although some escaped shipwreck.

In contrast, the great storm of October 1987, which caused such great and widespread damage ashore and to small craft in off-shore havens, resulted in very little loss of Channel shipping, evidence of the huge improvements in safety at sea that have been achieved in the last century.

Deal was once one of the four most prominent ports in the Kingdom. There never was a harbour there, but there was a naval dockyard which stretched from Deal Castle to the Time Ball Tower at Deal. It was The Downs that gave Deal its prominence and its prosperity. Sailing ships made Deal their last call for taking on fresh food and water for a long voyage and local boatmen made their living from transporting provisions, men and mail, out to the ships that lay at anchor there.

Those same boatmen were also noted for their piloting skills, for their readiness to aid in salvage work, 'sweeping' for lost anchors and cables which they then sold, and for all sorts of other marine odd jobs. All these activities were known as 'hovelling', and the hovellers' boats were the famous Deal luggers, 40 ft long, twin masted and with a crew of seven who slept in a little cabin forward. Charles Dickens said the Deal hovellers were 'among the bravest and most skilful mariners that exist' and, indeed, it was very high risk work that, in good

The front of Walmer lifeboat station, as seen from the main road through the town.

times, paid well. In less good times, it claimed many lives.

It was the arrival of steamships that led to the decline of Deal early in the 19th century. The steamships had no need to break their journeys in The Downs and after Dover was extended around 1850, the Deal trade was very badly hit. Many of the local boatmen, in fact, were forced to emigrate.

Today, Deal and its near neighbour Walmer have joined to form one urban seaside area, with the lifeboat station on Walmer Green. There, the lifeboat can be seen, from time to time, standing high on its launching platform on the beach in front of the lifeboat station, though today most of its life saving work is in the service of leisure sailors rather than working seafarers. A board on the outside of the building records that the Station was established in 1856 and closed in 1912. Then, in 1927, the RNLI decided to place a motor lifeboat at Walmer.

The board lists some of the Station highlights:

1944   Bronze medal awarded to Coxswain J Mercer for the rescue of 13 men from an anti-submarine boat.

1948   Coxswain Upton awarded the silver medal and Motor Mechanic C Cavell the bronze medal for the service to the vessel '*Silvia Onorato*' aground on Goodwin Sands. The rescue of 22 Italians, two German stowaways and one Alsatian dog took two days and nights in heavy seas and bitter cold.

1950   The bowman, James Rich, collapsed and died when the lifeboat went to the aid of the '*Santagata*' and rescued her crew of 32.

1952   Coxswain Upton was awarded a second silver medal and Motor Mechanic Cavell a bronze, for the service to the French steamer '*Agen*', aground on South Goodwin. By continuous manoeuvring the lifeboat was held against the wreck whilst 37 Frenchmen slid down ropes into the lifeboat.

1963   Inshore lifeboat placed on service on 18 April.

1969   The thanks of the Institution inscribed on vellum awarded to Helmsman Cyril Williams and crew members I Coe and C Taylor for the rescue of two men cut off by the tide.

1972   The thanks of the Institution inscribed on vellum awarded to Coxswain Henry Brown when the yacht '*Nell*', her crew of six and a cat were saved.

1977   The bronze medal awarded to Coxswain Bruce Brown when, having rescued the crew of 4 from the cabin cruiser '*Shark*', he boarded her shortly before she sank and rescued the second coxswain who had become trapped in the cabin.

1979   A letter of appreciation awarded to Acting Coxswain Williams for the rescue, in conjunction with the inshore lifeboat, of the crew of two from the yacht '*Jewel*'.

1985   A framed letter of appreciation awarded to Helmsman Anthony Evans for rescuing two men cut off from the tide.

1990   All weather lifeboat withdrawn on 6 May and replaced by the Atlantic 21 lifeboat '*US Navy League*'.

1991   The thanks of the Institution inscribed on vellum awarded to Helmsman Duane Brown of the Atlantic 21 lifeboat, for rescuing three crew from the yacht '*Jesse*'. Framed letters of appreciation were presented to crew members John Collins and Shaun East.

1992   Atlantic 21 lifeboat '*James Burgess*' placed on service.

Despite the reputation of the Goodwins, vessels beating up the Channel from south to north and heading for the Thames Estuary and the Port of London are not out of danger after they have rounded the North Foreland.

Much of the North Kent coast is actually in the Estuary, which is a delta of dangerous submerged sandbanks that include the Kentish Knock, the Sunk, East Barrow, West Barrow, Gunfleet, Red Sand, Margate Sand, the Longsand and many more. They, too, cause a confusion of tide and current that has been the undoing of many ships and more men down the years, adding significantly to the total of tragedy that can be attributed to the Kent coast.

An early shipwreck left an abiding mark on the North Kent coast. The ship was carrying two nuns who were travelling from the priory at Davington, just outside Faversham, to the minster that gave its name to the village on the bank of the Wantsum Channel that separated Thanet from mainland Kent.

That channel used to be a well-used short cut that avoided the need to follow the Thanet coast round to the great medieval port of Sandwich. Today, it is little more than a ditch, certainly not navigable, although still discernible.

According to legend, the Davington sisters were shipwrecked off the coast and one was drowned. The other was brought safely ashore at Reculver, a former Roman fortress guarding the northern end of the Wantsum Channel. There, in thanksgiving for her own salvation and in memory of her less fortunate sister, she caused a church to be built with a twin-tower gateway, just like that of the mother priory at Davington.

Davington Priory today has only one of the twin towers

remaining and the church at Reculver fell into disrepair and was vandalised until virtually nothing but the towers remained. They were adopted by Trinity House as a navigational landmark and stand today on the top of the low-rise cliffs, visible for some distance inland and much further out to sea.

Legend, too, claims that at least one of the vessels making up the mighty Spanish Armada was lost on the Goodwin Sands that day in July 1588 when the English ships followed the Spaniards past the Kent Channel ports on the way to Calais. History has very little to say about the claim, one way or the other, so it has to be stated with some caution at the very least.

Throughout the 20th century, ships continued to be wrecked off the Kent coast, though with decreasing frequency throughout the second half of the century, and the lifeboats still carry out their undaunted services. In the great storm of the century, the October 1987 'hurricane', the crew of Dover's 50 ft Thames class lifeboat *Rotary Service* braved conditions that hurled 50 ton stone blocks from the harbour breakwater into seas up to 60 ft high outside the harbour and 20 ft high inside, in order to go to the aid of the doomed bulk cargo vessel *Sumnia*. As a result of that service, Acting Coxswain Roy Couzens, who suffered a heart attack at sea and had to be rushed to hospital by his crew, was awarded the Royal National Lifeboat Institution's silver medal for gallantry. Other crew members were awarded the Institution's bronze medal for gallantry. Bronze medals were also awarded to members of the crew of the 44 ft Waveney class lifeboat *Helen Turnbull* of Sheerness for the rescue, during that same storm, of two men from a small vessel off the Isle of Grain, during which the lifeboat itself went aground and remained fast for almost 18 hours before her crew was able to free her and return to base.

No doubt, despite all the improvements in safety measures, the sea around the Kent coast will continue to take its toll of ships and crews during the 21st century just as it has done for more than a thousand years.

The Lifeboat is Coming!

For centuries, shipwreck was a constant possibility – indeed, for the habitual seagoer it was a real probability, faced by all seamen.

Shipwrecked mariners around the coast of Kent could hope their plight would be seen and recognised by boatmen in the towns of Walmer, Deal, Ramsgate, Broadstairs and Margate and that they would put out, often in the most daunting weather, to go to the aid of vessels ensnared by the dreaded Goodwin Sands or driven on to the coastal rocks and sandbanks.

But often, too, the wind and the sea daunted even these intrepid boatmen. Sometimes, even if they would have dared the elements, the conditions were such that they were simply physically incapable of launching their boats and getting them clear of the beaches. It was by no means unknown for brave and willing boatmen to have to stand on the shore and watch a wreck being pounded to pieces beneath the wretched survivors aboard her, while they were helpless to offer any kind of assistance at all.

In fact, it was just such an experience, in 18th century Newcastle, that spurred interest in efforts already being made to design a boat capable of enduring the roughest weather in order to go to the rescue of ships wrecked off the English coast.

In 1789, during a great gale at Newcastle, ships at sea ran for the shelter of the harbour. One, *Adventurer*, missed the harbour entrance and went on to nearby rocks. She was so close to the shore that thousands of people braved the force of the wind to stand on the pier, where they could only watch helplessly as, one by one, *Adventurer*'s crew were snatched from the ship's rigging and plunged to their deaths in the pounding surf or upon the rocks.

There was no hope of being able to launch a boat into that wind and those seas and the watchers on the shore could do nothing by way of responding to the desperate pleas for help that reached them all too clearly from the doomed crew. As a result of that experience, a committee was formed and prizes were offered for a lifeboat capable of making rescues in such conditions.

The idea of building such a boat was not new. A London coach-builder called Lionel Lukin had become interested in the problems of developing what he called 'an unsubmergible boat' several years before and had actually obtained a patent in November 1785 for his 'improved method of construction of boats and small vessels for either sailing or rowing which will neither over-set in violent gales or sudden bursts of wind nor sink if by any accident filled with water.'

Lukin was a native of Little Dunmow in Essex, where he was born on 18th May 1742. He became a member of the Coach-makers' Company in London in 1767, retired from business in 1824 and died in 1834, having by that time made his home at Hythe, in Kent.

His first 'unsubmergible boat' was a model which he tested on a pond at Dunmow and, encouraged by the interest shown in his experiments by the Prince of Wales (later George IV), Lukin bought a Norwegian yawl which he converted with a cork gunwale, air cases fore and aft and along the thwarts, and an iron plate added to the keel to provide greater strength and stability.

This was the idea he patented in 1785 and he sent the prototype, which he called *Experiment*, to Ramsgate to be

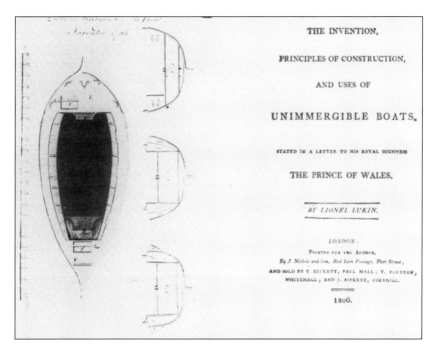

THE INVENTION,

PRINCIPLES OF CONSTRUCTION,

AND USES OF

UNIMMERGIBLE BOATS.

STATED IN A LETTER TO HIS ROYAL HIGHNESS

THE PRINCE OF WALES.

BY LIONEL LUKIN.

LONDON:

Printed for the Author,

By J. Nichols and Son, Red Lion Passage, Fleet Street;
AND SOLD BY T. BECKETT, PALL MALL; T. EGERTON,
WHITEHALL; AND J. ASPERNE, CORNHILL.

1806.

The title page of Lionel Lukin's description of his 'unimergible' boats. The importance of his work was not immediately recognised.

tested. The tests proved very successful. *Experiment* twice crossed the Channel when other vessels would not venture out, but then word reached Lukin that his boat had proved so successful that she had been used for smuggling and had been confiscated.

Undeterred, he built another boat, a 20-footer called *Witch*, which he also had tested in rough weather off the Kent coast, this time by naval officers at Margate. Word of his work travelled and Lukin was asked to adapt a Northumbrian coble for use as a lifeboat at Bamburgh. He carried out the commission and the boat was in service by 1778.

16

The gravestone of Lionel Lukin in Hythe churchyard. On the reverse is inscribed, 'This Lionel Lukin was the first who built a lifeboat and was the first inventor of that principle of safety by which many lives and much property have been preserved from shipwrecks.'

Lukin was the first man to realise the need for different boats for different coasts. He wrote: 'It is particularly advisable that all lifeboats should be built of the form most approved by the pilots and seamen of the coast where they are to be used as no one form will fit all shores.'

After his death, a memorial window was unveiled to his memory in Hythe parish church and his grave in Hythe churchyard is inscribed: 'This Lionel Lukin was the first who built a Lifeboat and was the first inventor of that principle of safety by which many lives and much property have been preserved from shipwreck. . . .'

The other side of the headstone relates: 'In this grave is interred the body of Lionel Lukin – born at Dunmow in Essex the 18th of May 1742 – in 1767 he became a member of the Coach Maker's Company of London and after 60 years of various success in that business – settled at Hythe in 1824 with the humble hope that the same Divine Providence which had been his guide and protector during a long and chequered life would permit him to conclude it in ease and tranquillity and finally remove him to a better and eternal inheritance through the merits and intercession of Christ Jesus our Redeemer – died the 16th of February 1834.'

The worth of his lifeboat design was not immediately and universally recognised. Despite Royal patronage, their Lordships of the Admiralty and the Master of Trinity House were not impressed. Their Lordships said they had never heard of such a thing as an 'unimergible' boat and they did not bother to inquire any further about it. To them, the description was self-evidently absurd.

Nevertheless, five more boats were built to Lukin's design and as a result of the competition that was launched after the *Adventurer* shipwreck off Newcastle in 1789, new designs were submitted by two men. One was painter William Wouldhave; the other, boat-builder Henry Greathead of South Shields.

Wouldhave's design was simply for a boat containing a great

deal of cork. Greathead proposed a boat with a curved instead of a straight keel and fitted with seven hundredweight of cork, but no air boxes.

It was Greathead's design that won the award and although he did not patent it he did receive a Parliamentary grant with which to build a boat to his design. In 1789 the Duke of Northumberland ordered one to be built at his expense by Greathead and he provided an annuity for its maintenance after it was stationed at North Shields. After that, Greathead received several orders for lifeboats and by 1803 there were five in operation in Scotland and 18 in England.

By now there was a growing recognition throughout the country of a need not just for boats capable of surviving the worst weather at sea but for a co-ordinated regular lifeboat service using such boats. British seaborne trade had increased enormously and more ships meant, inevitably, more ship-wrecks. The Government could not be persuaded that a natio-nal lifeboat service was needed, but many people were saying it was no longer good enough for the lives of seamen and their passengers to be saved or lost according to whether or not the particular part of the coast on which their ship was wrecked had an adequately supported lifeboat.

One of those men was a leading lifeboatman of Douglas, Isle of Man. He was Sir William Hillary who, with the help of supporters, including some Members of Parliament, set up the National Institution for the Preservation of Life from Ship-wreck. It was the forerunner of the Royal National Lifeboat Institution, which adopted that title in 1854.

Hillary opened lifeboat stations on the Isle of Man and himself won the Institution's gold medal for gallantry three times for services with the Douglas lifeboat. By 1824 he had helped to rescue more than 300 people from death at sea and he understood very well just how necessary was a national lifeboat service.

At that time there were 39 serviceable lifeboats, 25 of them

19

Greathead's winning lifeboat, designed in response to a competition launched after the tragic shipwreck of the *Adventurer* off Newcastle in 1789.

provided by Lloyd's of London and the rest by local benefactors and charitable organisations. There was little or no co-operation or co-ordination of their services, however, and there were not enough lifeboats to meet the ever-growing need.

Some of the local organisations joined the new Institution, but once the initial enthusiasm waned, the project began to decline again. By 1850 there were only 19 lifeboats connected with the service. Many boats had been so neglected through lack of voluntary support and funds that they were no longer serviceable.

In an effort to rekindle enthusiasm, the Duke of Northumberland offered a prize of 100 guineas for the best model lifeboat. Among the specifications he stipulated, the boat had to be self-righting and self-emptying, light enough to be capable of being transported overland from one place to another when necessary, and not too expensive.

20

The competition excited the imaginations of inventors all over the world but the prize went to James Beeching of Great Yarmouth in Norfolk. He built a boat which he called *Northumberland* and which, when tested, proved to be very successful.

Like Lukin's first lifeboat, *Northumberland* was tested at Ramsgate and was put to the test over the Goodwin Sands. It was designed to be propelled by either (or both) sail and oars and in 1851 it was bought by Trinity House for the use of the Royal Harbour at Ramsgate. The design was subsequently improved upon but this was the boat that is still today regarded as the first of the modern lifeboats.

In 1851 there were 91 lifeboats, of which 30 were under the administration of the Institution, but gradually this figure increased until by 1891 most local lifeboat organisations had joined the RNLI and there were 300 lifeboats stationed around the British coast.

From 1854 until 1869 the RNLI received a government grant but the Institution relinquished this because the conditions imposed by the government were unpopular with local stations and the grant itself also affected voluntary contributions which were still needed.

The RNLI is still wholly supported by voluntary funds today. In 2001, it expected its costs to amount to some £95 million.

Now, there are more than 311 large and smaller lifeboats at 224 stations, and a relief fleet of more than 40 all-weather boats that can replace station boats when they have to have their periodic inspections, surveys or repairs. Since its foundation in 1824, RNLI lifeboats have saved more than 135,000 lives.

Today, many of the services are to leisure craft in difficulties rather than to merchantmen in distress, but almost always lives are at risk and it is always with heartfelt relief that crews still echo the cry of generations of thankful seagoers: 'It's going to be all right – the lifeboat is coming!'

'None But Englishmen . . .'

The night of Monday, 5th January 1857 was such a night as sailors yarn about – afterwards.

It was a night of howling gale and freezing spray in which ships cowered, if they could, in coastal havens, their naked masts clawing at the clouds as though seeking a hold by which to steady themselves, their rigging shrieking in agony as the wind did its best to tear it free.

Certainly, it was no night in which to be beating up the English Channel, knowing that the Goodwin Sands waited greedily to feast on yet another passing morsel should it be hapless enough to be driven into their unrelenting embrace. Several ships were wrecked on or near the Kent coast that night and more further along the east and south coasts, as well.

The crew of the American barque *Northern Belle*, a vessel of 1,000 tons bound from New York to London, knew very well the dangers of such a night as they tried to force their way round the North Foreland. The wind was blowing from the north-east and they were being driven closer and closer to the rocks below the cliffs.

At last, about 3 a.m., the master of the *Northern Belle* gave the order to drop anchor and she came to a halt about three-quarters of a mile off Kingsgate, between Margate and the North Foreland.

It was not the best part of the Thanet coastline in which to be anchored in a north-easterly gale which threatened every moment to pluck the ship from her tenuous safety and hurl her upon the coastal rocks. But, despite the huge buffeting of the mountainous seas which frequently broke over her deck and threatened to take her to the bottom under the sheer weight of water that crashed down upon her, the *Northern Belle* rode at anchor there throughout the rest of that fearful night.

At six o'clock the next morning, three Margate luggers, *Ocean*, *Eclipse* and *Victory*, put out to give whatever help they could to the crew of the *Northern Belle*, whose danger was fully appreciated by the Kent seamen. *Ocean* succeeded in getting close enough to put five men aboard, while the other two luggers stood by ready to offer any further aid that might be called for.

At 6.30, her crew cut away the mizzen and main masts to lighten her and she did, in fact, ride rather easier after that. But the gale had not yet tired of its plaything. As the sky lightened, just a little, with the coming of day, the storm increased its force and the sea ran even higher than before.

By 8 a.m. it was thought impossible that the anchor cables could take the enormous strain without parting, in which case the *Northern Belle* would surely be driven on to the rocks and wrecked. Watchers on the shore realised there was little chance that she could hold her own against the gale for much longer and a message was sent to Broadstairs to launch the lifeboat and go to the rescue.

Three times the crew of the lifeboat *Mary White* tried to launch their boat into the surf. Three times they were hurled back. But there are more ways of getting a lifeboat into the sea than by defying a gale head-on.

'We shall have to manhandle her round to Kingsgate,' the coxswain shouted above the howling gale. 'There will be more protection there and we should be able to get her out. We'll need some volunteers.'

There was already a small crowd out watching the efforts of the lifeboat to get launched and many of the men knew exactly what was needed. With little hesitation, they helped haul the lifeboat back out of the surf and on to her launching trolley. Then, they harnessed themselves to the ropes attached to the trolley and, straining into the wind and against the deadweight of the boat and the wetness of the ground, they began the two mile haul over the North Foreland and across the fields to Kingsgate Bay.

The lifeboat arrived at Kingsgate at about 9 a.m. By that time, the news of the operation had spread and, despite the violence of the storm, a crowd of several hundred people from Margate, Ramsgate and Broadstairs had assembled on the cliff tops to watch the rescue attempt.

At 11.30, the huddled spectators watched as the lugger *Victory* was hit by an enormous sea that bowled her completely over and bore her down under its weight. They gasped, holding their breath in hope of seeing the little vessel rise again, but she did not. She sank to the bottom, taking her crew of nine men with her. They included two father and son couples. The men aboard *Ocean* saw what happened to *Victory* and tried to go to her assistance, nearly suffering a similar fate in the attempt. But it was too late. There were no survivors from the *Victory*.

As the morning wore on, the plight of the *Northern Belle* became more and more desperate and by noon it was expected every moment that the ship's anchor cables must part at last and she would be driven on to the rocks.

All through the day the watchers on the shore waited and all through the day the *Northern Belle* clung doggedly to her anchorage, defying the gale which now added hail, sleet and snow to its armoury with which to attack the defenceless ship.

It was between 10 and 11 p.m. when the ship finally succumbed. Her anchor cables, tested to the limit, at last parted and the ship was hurled by the triumphant storm upon the waiting rocks at the foot of the cliffs of Kingsgate Bay.

By now it was quite impossible to launch the lifeboat. The darkness of the night was full of sleet and snow and visibility was very limited indeed. The place from which the lifeboat would have to be launched was more than half a mile from where the *Northern Belle* was beached on the rocks. There was nothing anyone could do until next morning.

Aboard the wrecked barque, the crew and the Margate men from the lugger *Ocean*, climbed into the rigging of the one remaining mast and lashed themselves there, above the worst of the seas that broke over the decks, from which they would certainly have been washed if they had remained there. They were still, however, at the mercy of the freezing spray and wind-driven snow that reached up to saturate their clothes and ice their beards and hair.

That night was even worse than the night before for the men aboard the *Northern Belle*. But they survived it and when day broke on Tuesday, the crowd that again gathered along the cliff tops to watch the renewed rescue effort could clearly see the 23 men clinging to the rigging of the wreck. So near – and yet so far . . .

It was not until half past seven that the lifeboat, the *Mary White*, could at last be launched. The boat had been presented to Broadstairs boatmen by Mr Thomas White of Cowes, Isle of Wight, in July 1850, and had already saved many lives around this corner of the Kent coast. With her ten man crew, the boat was pulled through the surf and out into the still violent sea. She reached the wreck and seven of the men aboard were taken off into the boat.

In the course of the rescue, however, the lifeboat became entangled in wreckage and might have been dashed to pieces against the much greater bulk of the ship if she had not been cut free. It meant the rest of the ship's crew had to be left where they were while the lifeboat returned to the shore where the survivors she had taken on board were landed safely, their chilled bones warmed as much by the welcome they were given by the assembled crowd as by the knowledge that they, at least, were safe and that there were now increased hopes for the

After rescuing the crew of the American vessel, *The Northern Belle*, the crew of the lifeboat *The Mary White* returned to a tumultuous reception by the people of Broadstairs.

eventual rescue of the remainder of the barque's crew.

A second lifeboat, the *Culmer White*, which had also been wheeled from Broadstairs to be ready in case disaster befell the first, was launched. She, too, reached the wreck and brought away another 14 of the men left on board.

Only two men now remained aboard the wreck: the captain and the pilot, who had been taken on at Dover. The captain declared he preferred to die aboard his ship rather than desert her. The pilot said he would remain with the Captain.

The lifeboat landed the 14 men safely and, after an hour and a half, put out again in a last attempt to persuade the remaining two men on board the *Northern Belle* to recognise the pointlessness of their proposed sacrifice. What arguments they employed were never made public, but at last the persuasiveness of the lifeboatmen succeeded, and the two men finally agreed to leave the doomed vessel. To renewed cheers from the watching

26

crowds, they climbed into the lifeboat and were brought ashore to join the rest of the crew.

All 23 survivors from the *Northern Belle* were taken to the Captain Digby, the inn that stands on the cliff at Kingsgate, where no doubt they restored their spirits in time-honoured fashion.

The rescue mission successfully concluded, at 3 p.m. that day the lifeboat *Mary White* was dragged on her trolley back to Broadstairs, not by volunteer manpower this time, but by three horses. In the boat were her crew, who held aloft an oar from the American vessel's boat, to which was tied that same American flag which had been flown, upside down, as a distress signal when the barque was still straining at her anchors out in the bay.

The crowd of jubilant spectators marched along beside the boat, cheering all the way back to Broadstairs, where they were joined by half the people of the little Kent town, who formed a procession with the boat and its heroes at the centre. There and then, subscriptions began to be made to a fund to reward the lifeboatmen for their efforts and to succour the widows and orphans of the men lost in the lugger, *Victory*.

The rescue of the crew of the *Northern Belle* inspired a poem of seven verses by Charles Mackay which was published in the *Illustrated London News* of 17th January 1887. It was called, reasonably enough, *The Shipwreck of the Northern Belle*, and the last verse referred to those men of the lugger *Victory* who died – 'the noble nine' – and called upon the country to help their widows and orphans.

For the record, the crew of the *Mary White* lifeboat were John Castle, George Castle, William Hiller (Jnr), Robert Hiller, James Rowe, George Emptage and Edward Emptage.

The *Culmer White*, on her first trip to the *Northern Belle*, was crewed by John Cowell, William Wales, Jethrow Hiller, John Sandwell, George Emptage, Thomas Holborn, William Ralph, Robert Gilbert and Robert Parker. On her second trip,

27

from which she brought back the captain and the pilot, the *Culmer White* had aboard John Cowell, William Wales, Jethrow Hiller, Jerry Walker, Fred Lawrence, Thomas Sandwell, Robert Simpson, Jarvis Bell, Robert Parker, George Emptage and Alfred Emptage.

It was afterwards reported that the second mate of the *Northern Belle*, a man of English descent, told anyone who would listen to him as he and his shipmates burned out the memories of two terrible nights in Kingsgate Bay with toddy and grog in the parlour of the Captain Digby, that none but Englishmen could have put off to the rescue in such a sea as they had cheated that day.

Once More Into The Spray!

∽◇∾

For more than a week, from Saturday, 16th October through to Tuesday, 26th October 1869, a succession of terrific gales pounded the Kent coast, first from the south and then veering round to north-north-west.

Many vessels sought the time-honoured protection of The Downs, and among them was the *Frank Shaw*, a vessel of some 900 tons, bound from Shields for Genoa with a cargo of coal and coke. There she lay, sheltered it was true, but still buffeted by a wind that threatened to tear her from her anchors and bear her out on to the waiting Goodwin Sands.

At last, her master decided his only safety lay in slipping the anchors and seeking a still more secure haven off the North Foreland. But, that done, the *Frank Shaw* was riding very heavily in the stormy weather on Tuesday morning, 19th October, with her decks being swept by water fore and aft and everything that was not adequately secured being washed away.

With more and more water finding its way below decks, overwhelming the pumps, the ship was gradually but perceptibly settling deeper in the water. To remain where she was, anchored and at the mercy of every vicious wave that clawed its way across her defenceless decks and with no indication that the terrible weather would improve, was to invite inevitable disaster and so it was decided to slip her anchor for a second time and let the ship run before the wind in an attempt to reach Dover and the safety of the harbour there.

But visibility was poor and as the *Frank Shaw*, heavy with water, floundered south along the Kent coast, her master could not make out the buoys that would guide him through the lurking sandbanks. At about two o'clock in the afternoon, the thing he most dreaded happened. The *Frank Shaw* struck on the North Sands Head and was held fast.

The huge seas swept clean over the stranded vessel with enormous force and within a quarter of an hour she had broken in two. Her masts, sails and rigging were all washed away. All hands crowded to the after end of the deck for safety and distress signals were made.

Her plight had already been recognised by watchers at Broadstairs even before she struck the Sands, and the lifeboat was got ready. Almost as soon as the *Frank Shaw* went on to the Sands, the lifeboat was launched. The Ramsgate lifeboat was equally ready but there was some delay in launching her, with the result that the two lifeboats arrived at the Sands more or less together at about 3.30.

The seas were so huge and so rough that the boats could not get near the wreck, but a line was thrown from the ship to one of the boats, which secured it. However, the constant snatch and strain as the boats surged towards each other and were hurled apart again broke the line and by four o'clock the crew of the *Frank Shaw* were despairing of rescue. The lifeboatmen, though, had a trick or two up their sleeves yet.

As the tide fell, both lifeboats grounded on the Sands to leeward of the ship, which offered some protection from the unabating storm as, at about five o'clock, the crew of the *Frank Shaw* prepared to launch their gig in an attempt to cross the shallow water that separated them from the lifeboats.

The sea was not to be that easily cheated of its prey. The gig was smashed by the force of the waves before it could be manned and pulled away from the ship. Once again, the raised hopes of the now desperate crew were dashed.

Another boat was launched, more successfully this time, and

six of the ship's crew got into her and brought her to where the Sands were now uncovered by the low tide. Unable to row to the lifeboats because there was not enough water, the men left their boat where it was and waded to the Broadstairs lifeboat.

Heartened by their success, the men still on board the wreck tried to pull the ship's boat back to the *Frank Shaw* for more survivors, but the heavy surf caught it up, slammed it down on to the sand and stove it in, making it useless and depriving the rest of the crew of the *Frank Shaw* of yet another route to rescue.

The ship's carpenter was then equipped with a lifebuoy and sent to fight his way through the boat-battering surf on to the firm sand and thence to the waiting lifeboats. When he made the 200-yard journey safely, the rest of the crew, led by the pilot, a man from Deal, jumped overboard and began to wade towards the two waiting lifeboats.

The current ran across the Sands very strongly, so that the water through which they waded was rushing round their legs at between six and eight knots. Several of the men were swept away and finally only one of the men that tried to reach the Ramsgate lifeboat, *Bradford*, actually did so. Thirteen made it safely to the Broadstairs boat.

Even then their ordeal was not over, because the two lifeboats were still fast upon the Sands and they had to wait in the pounding surf until the tide turned and enabled the boats to float off and make their way back to the Ramsgate tug which was standing by to take them in tow. It was almost ten o'clock that evening before the lifeboats, with the survivors aboard, were finally towed back to the safety of their home port.

By this time, a large crowd of onlookers had gathered on Ramsgate pier to await the outcome of the rescue attempt and when the tug steamed alongside, a great cheer went up. The shipwrecked sailors were just about exhausted by their ordeal and had to be almost carried bodily by the crowd to the Sailors' Home for food, drink and a much needed rest.

31

The lifeboatmen, too, were very tired, but for them the day was not yet over. Just before they reached the harbour, signal rockets were sighted from the Gull lightship and from yet another vessel aground on the Goodwins. As soon as the Ramsgate lifeboat had discharged its human cargo, it was at once manned by a fresh crew, except for Cox'n Jarman, who again put to sea in tow of the tug, *Aid*.

Despite a search of the Sands, they found no wreck this time and returned home shortly after 2 a.m. on Wednesday, by which time the wind had increased to near hurricane force. It was assumed that the other, still unidentified, vessel had been lost with all hands on the Goodwins.

The *Frank Shaw* lost eight men drowned. The rest, including the Deal pilot, were saved. The ship itself was pounded to pieces in a very short time and by Wednesday morning, scarcely more than twelve hours after the crew was rescued, nothing remained of her to be seen.

She was just one more wreck consumed completely by the insatiable appetite of the voracious Goodwin Sands.

Women and Children First!

If it is possible to describe one shipwreck as a greater or lesser tragedy than any other, then certainly one of the worst ever to occur off the Kent coast was the loss of the wooden emigrant ship *Northfleet*, off Dungeness on 22nd January, 1873.

The *Northfleet* took her name from the Thames-side town where she was built in 1853: a full-rigged ship of some 876 tons, with a newly re-coppered bottom. When she left Gravesend at about 6 a.m. on Friday, 17th January in tow of the London steam tug *Middlesex*, she was commanded by her former Chief Officer, Edward Knowles. It was his first command, although he had sailed under *Northfleet*'s usual master, Capt Thomas Oates, for some years.

Capt Oates would have been in command for this voyage to Hobart, Tasmania, too, if he had not been ordered, literally at the last moment before sailing, to leave the ship and attend court to give evidence at the famous Tichbourne Trial, he having been probably the last man to see the real Sir Roger Tichbourne in Rio.

Knowles, a Gravesend man, had been married only six weeks to his wife Frederica, who had been given permission by the owners to accompany her husband on this voyage. For the rest, *Northfleet* had a crew of 34 men and she carried 343 passengers, many of them railway workers and their families making the journey in order to work on the new railway which was then being laid in Tasmania. The ship was also carrying about 450 tons of cargo, most of it iron for tracks and other railway materials.

After she left Gravesend, the *Northfleet* met the full force of the storm that raged in the open sea beyond the Thames Estuary and many of her passengers suffered badly from sea-sickness, so that the ship's surgeon was kept busy looking after them, particularly the women.

Accompanied by his new bride, Captain Edward Knowles took up his first command on what was to be *Northfleet*'s last voyage.

The ship was towed to Dungeness, where the tug cast off and the ship spread her sails in an attempt to beat her way through the Channel into the gale. By this time it was night and the *Northfleet* butted into the headwind until 7 a.m. on Sunday, by which time the gale was so strong the ship was making no headway at all and her master decided to turn back and seek shelter further up the coast.

At about 3 p.m. on Sunday, 19th January, therefore, the ship dropped anchor in Margate Roads and she remained there until 9 a.m. the next day. The weather had moderated somewhat by then and the wind had shifted to the north-west, so again *Northfleet* shaped a course down-Channel. But as she passed Folkestone, the wind veered to the south-west again and freshened to gale force. Frustrated, Capt Knowles bore up for Dungeness and, on Wednesday, 22nd January, he once again dropped anchor, in some eleven fathoms of water, between two and three miles off Dungeness, almost opposite the Coastguard station there.

By ten o'clock that night, most of the passengers had taken to their bunks and it was approaching 11 p.m. when the men on watch, two men and a petty officer, saw an unidentified outward bound steamer coming straight for them at full speed. They hailed the steamer, asking who she was and where she was bound, their voices rising as the oncoming vessel showed no sign of slowing or altering course.

The noise of their cries aroused Capt Knowles and the pilot, George Brack, who were both below. They hurried up on to the deck, arriving just as the steamer, still unidentified, hit the *Northfleet* broadside, almost amidship, on the starboard side. The impact holed her below the waterline and crushed the massive transverse timbers of the wooden sailing ship.

Immediately, despite desperate cries from the people aboard *Northfleet*, the steamer made all haste to get clear of her victim. Before more than a few of the terrified passengers could rush up from their quarters below, many still clad in their night clothes,

35

she was already completely out of sight, offering no assistance nor remaining to find out what damage had been done.

Aboard *Northfleet*, there was panic among the passengers as Capt Knowles ordered distress rockets to be fired and boats to be launched. The ship's signal gun malfunctioned and would not fire, but flares were burned.

The starboard lifeboat was lowered, with Bosun John Easter in charge. The captain's young wife, Frederica, wanted to stay at her husband's side, but he kissed her and gently but firmly persuaded her into the boat with a lifebelt round her. He had to threaten to shoot any of the navvies who did not obey his order to stand back and let the women and children get away first, but one of the men shouted that he'd as soon be shot as drowned and rushed the boat.

Knowles fired a shot over the men's heads and, when that had no effect, he shot a man in the leg. Ironically, the wounded man was one of those who were saved.

Despite the shot, twelve men jumped into the boat as it was being lowered and she was stove in. She was taking in a lot of water and Knowles, with a 'God bless you!' farewell, ordered the half-filled boat to shove off and to row as fast as it could to the nearest vessel. Some men in the water clung to her sides, threatening to overturn her, and the bosun threatened to chop off their hands if they did not let go.

As the boat pulled away from the wreck, some of those left aboard took to the rigging. One of them was the Trinity House pilot, George Brack. But almost at once, the ship foundered, throwing them, too, into the sea. Mr Brack managed to cling to the top of the mast, which remained sticking up above the water, until he was picked up some time later.

Although there were almost a hundred other vessels at anchor in the vicinity that night, none of them seems to have realised that *Northfleet* was in any kind of distress. Her signals were read by the other crews as a summons for a pilot and it was some 20 minutes or half an hour before anyone realised that anything was amiss. It was a dark and squally night with a light drizzle falling, but the shore lights were clearly visible and the sea was not too rough for any of the other ships to have launched boats to go to the aid of *Northfleet* if her plight had been understood. If they had done so, all the people aboard might well have been saved.

By the time the boat with the captain's wife and other survivors had cleared *Northfleet*, water was pouring into the ship through a broached hull and, despite all the pumps could do, her figurehead dipped below the surface. Her stern, crowded with terrified passengers and crew, lifted into the air before, with a loud rushing noise, it followed the prow below the surface, leaving several hundred people struggling for their lives in the bitterly cold water.

Within 20 or 30 minutes of the collision, the *Northfleet* had sunk in 66 ft of water, leaving just the tops of her masts still showing above the surface. The cries of the men and the shrieks of the women and children could be heard several miles away until, one by one, they were silenced by the cold and by exhaustion. Some clung to bits of floating wreckage, but most of them, too, were soon swept away and drowned.

By this time, the steam tug *City of London*, commanded by Capt Samuel Kingston, had reached the scene, having sighted the distress signals. The tug had been at anchor, waiting for work, and Capt Kingston at first thought *Northfleet*'s flares were signals for a pilot. But on second thoughts he decided to investigate anyway and he found the lifeboat with Mrs Knowles and the other women in it. He took them aboard and the little lifeboat went back towards the wreck to rescue four more survivors, who were also brought to safety aboard the steamer. The tug remained cruising in the vicinity throughout the rest of the night, picking up any survivors who had been able to get clear of the wreck and remain afloat. In fact, the tug saved 34 people altogether.

Another 32 were saved by the Kingsdown lugger *Mary*,

which also answered the distress signals, and more were rescued by other vessels that hurried to the scene. The *Princess*, from Dover, succeeded in taking off 21 people, ten of them from the *Northfleet*'s rigging, including the pilot, George Brack.

When the final count was taken, 86 of all those people who had been aboard the *Northfleet* were rescued. They were cared for at the National Sailors' Home at Dover, except for Mrs Knowles, who was housed overnight with a local clergyman. Of 248 men steerage passengers, 71 survived; of 42 women, only one. Of 44 children aged between one and twelve years, only one survived, and so did one of the eight infants aboard. Eleven of her crew of 34, and Mrs Knowles, were also saved. The rest, including Capt Knowles, who remained aboard and went down with his ship, were lost.

Lloyd's of London sent telegrams to places all along the Kent coast asking for information of others rescued and providing food and clothing for all survivors at the company's expense. Many bodies were later washed up on the coast from Lydd to St Margaret's Bay and were buried locally.

A public subscription was founded for the relatives of those lost aboard the *Northfleet*, to which Queen Victoria subscribed £200, and within a short time the fund contained several thousand pounds. There were 85 people to be provided for from the fund, including a ten year old girl, Maria Taplin, who lost both her parents, a brother and a sister in that one calamitous night. She was taken the following day by Mrs Knowles to be looked after by relatives in London.

A preliminary inquiry was held at the Custom House, Dover, the following afternoon and the Board of Trade offered £100 reward for information about the offending steamer, which had quit the scene still unidentified. Several vessels came under suspicion, but eventually it became clear that the most likely culprit was a Spanish steamer called *Murillo*, which had left Antwerp for Lisbon and which was at first supposed to have sunk almost immediately after colliding with *Northfleet*.

In fact, however, the *Murillo* survived the collision with very little damage and arrived in Cadiz during the evening of Thursday, 30th January, having stopped at Belem, the entrance to the port of Lisbon, the day before. There, she had received a telegram telling her to continue to Cadiz without discharging any of her cargo at Lisbon.

At Cadiz, the British Consul insisted upon an inquiry and it was found that her starboard bow had been newly painted black and red to the waterline. Her port bow was dented, but her owners insisted that the painting was done in London or Antwerp before she started on her voyage to Cadiz and the dent was caused two years before as she was entering the port of Le Havre. Nevertheless, the master and crew were arrested and detained while an investigation went ahead.

Two Englishmen, a passenger called Samuel Bell and the *Murillo*'s second engineer, James Goodeave, who had shared a cabin, swore they had heard noises aboard the steamer as if something unusual was happening and they said they had felt a slight shock of collision, too. They thought the shock was so slight because the steamer's engines were already in reverse at the time of the collision.

Both said they distinctly heard the cries of women and children but although they tried to make the Spaniards understand the need to stop and lower boats, they sailed away from the scene.

The *Murillo* was a vessel of 300 tons, designed and built at Glasgow but Spanish owned. By a strange irony, she was a successor to another vessel of the same name, built by the same shipyard for the same owners, which was run down and sunk by an unknown steamer almost exactly where the *Northfleet* sank in November 1864. Several lives were lost and no culprit was ever named.

Like the *Northfleet*, the *Murillo* had sailed without her usual captain, Capt Marc, who so similarly to Capt Oates, had been summoned to give evidence in a court case. The steamer was, at

39

The Spanish steamer *Murillo*, which collided with and sunk the *Northfleet*. Although the cries of the passengers could be heard on board, the steamer sailed away from the scene, without offering help.

the time of the *Northfleet* disaster, under command of Felipe Berrute, who had been First Mate under Capt Marc for some time. It was said that if *Murillo* had remained on her course that night of 22nd January, she would have run aground on Dungeness Point. Instead, though, she changed course, hit *Northfleet*, and continued on her way.

Northfleet's victims were buried in churchyards nearest to the point on the coast where they were washed up: Lydd, New Romney, Worth and St Margaret's. At Lydd a new piece of ground for burial had to be hurriedly consecrated.

A memorial window in New Romney's St Nicholas' church has an inscription: 'The dead shall hear the voice of the Son of God and they that hear shall live. In memory of the crew and passengers of the ship *Northfleet* which foundered off the coast 22 January 1873.'

Two reforms resulted from the *Northfleet* disaster. A recognised system of distress signals became compulsory so that never again would distress signals be mistaken for a request for a pilot; and it became a legal requirement for all British ships to have the name painted on both bows.

For Conspicuous Gallantry

◈

The Quebec-built three-master *Indian Chief*, owned and registered in Liverpool, made her last voyage from India in 1880 and discharged her cargo in London before sailing north to pick up a fresh cargo of more than a thousand tons of pig and bar iron and 200 casks of soda for delivery to Yokahama.

She left Middlesborough, under the command of Capt Marmaduke Fraser, early in the morning of 2nd January, 1881 and, with a pilot aboard to see her safely to Beachy Head, she set off down the English east coast. It should have been a routine passage southwards across the Thames Estuary, through the Straits of Dover and into the Channel. There, off the Sussex white cliffs, she would have paid off the pilot and headed south into the open sea.

At a little before midnight on 5th January, the pilot sighted the shore lights of Orfordness (Suffolk) some seven miles off on the starboard bow and he set his course for the Kentish Knock lightship. The ship's mate, Mr Lloyd, went aloft to keep a lookout for the lightship. When he came down again it was to report that he had sighted a light dead ahead.

'Must be the Kentish Knock,' he told the captain, who agreed with him. The pilot, however, was not so sure.

'We shouldn't have sighted the Knock yet,' he argued. 'No, I reckon what you saw must have been some fisherman, not the lightship at all.'

The captain shrugged. 'If you say so.' He gave the order to

42

put the ship about to go on to the starboard tack, continuing her way along the coast.

As the helm was put down to bring the ship round, the main brace fouled and in the momentary confusion that followed, with the vessel heeling hard over, a flailing rope tangled itself round the wheel. Temporarily, the vessel was out of control and it was some little time before the confusion ended and she was brought under full control again on the starboard tack.

Just as everything seemed to be settling back to normal again, the ship struck ground, broadside on, and juddered to an abrupt halt. It was 2.30 a.m. on 5th January, 1881 and the *Indian Chief* was fast upon the Long Sand off Margate.

At once, Capt Fraser ordered rockets to be fired and flares to be burned so that nearby lightships would know there was a vessel in distress. Then he told the crew: 'Better get below until help arrives. There's nothing more we can do on deck.'

When dawn broke, some of the crew sighted what they at first thought must be the sail of a lifeboat in the distance. In fact, though, it was the fishing smack *Increase*, out of Walton on the Naze, about a mile away from *Indian Chief*. Her skipper saw the stranded vessel but when he trained his glass on her he could see no sign of life. He made signals, but there were no replies so, after remaining in the vicinity for a couple of hours, just in case, he went away again, assuming all those on board the grounded vessel must have abandoned her before he arrived.

During the day, as the tide ebbed, the *Indian Chief* broke her back amidships across the sandbanks on which she was held. Recognising that his ship was lost now, Capt Fraser's main concern was for the safety of all aboard. He gave the order to abandon ship and the lifeboats were lowered into heavy seas.

The first, with only two members of the crew aboard, was instantly swept away and was lost. Two other boats filled with water as soon as they were lowered and became unserviceable. The rest of the crew was marooned on board the broken vessel.

When the ship broke her back, the mainmast was weakened

and on the captain's advice some of the men took to the mizzenmast. Some, however, climbed the foremast, lashing themselves to the rigging where they settled down as best they could in the miserably cold and wet conditions to await rescue, as darkness fell.

Before he joined them, Capt Fraser gave his watch and chain to his mate, with a message to take home to his family for him if the worst happened. The mate was one of those who chose the mizzenmast for his refuge but later on he changed his mind and joined the crewmen on the foremast. That move saved his life.

At about 3 a.m. on 6th January, a heavy sea swept away the weakened mainmast and took with it the mizzenmast and all the men lashed to it, including Capt Fraser. Securely tied into position and too frozen to free themselves, they stood no chance at all and were all drowned.

Twelve men remained on board the wreck, all of them roped to the remaining foremast. There seemed very little reason for them to hope that their fate would not be the same as that of their shipmates, for there was no sign of any rescue attempt. It could, they were all sure in their hearts, be only a matter of time.

Unknown to them, however, their rockets and flares had been seen by the Sunk lightship, but they had been misunderstood. The lightship crew thought they were signals made by a ship needing a pilot.

It was not until dawn the next day, 6th January, that the crew of the lightship made out the *Indian Chief* and realized she was aground on the Long Sand. They at once followed normal procedure, sending off two carrier pigeons to Harwich, each carrying the signal letters BDG, the international code for Vessel on Shore. They hoisted the same BDG flag signal, too, and fired two signal guns at half-hourly intervals. There was no more they could do. They were not to know it would take the two pigeons two days to reach their home loft at Harwich.

By coincidence, two hours before *Indian Chief* ran aground, a steamship, *Nymphaea*, bound from North Shields to Athens, had also gone aground. The *Nymphaea* was fast on the east side of the Sunk Sand. She, too, sent up distress signals which were seen, at just about the time the *Indian Chief* was grounding, by a fishing smack at anchor near the Gunfleet. The smack got under way in an effort to reach the *Nymphaea*, but was unable to do so in the very heavy seas that were running.

But at 5.30 a.m., the men aboard the smack saw flares from *Indian Chief* and bore towards her. They were within about three-quarters of a mile of her when they sighted another smack, *Aquiline*, coming out of the Goldmere Gap. The two crews of the fishing vessels agreed between them that *Aquiline* should go directly to Harwich, bring out the lifeboat and also telegraph for help from other lifeboat stations along the coast.

While *Aquiline* was hurrying to Harwich with her message for the lifeboat to go to the aid of *Nymphaea*, another smack, *Forget-me-not*, saw the Knock lightship's signal. Her skipper went to the lightship and was told that the *Indian Chief* was ashore on the Long Sand. He at once headed back for Ramsgate, arriving there just before noon.

Although *Aquiline* reach Harwich at 11 a.m. and the lifeboat was ready for sea by 11.30, it could not put out without the help of the steam tug and that had to get up steam first. So it was not until one o'clock in the afternoon that the Harwich lifeboat, *Springwell*, was able to set out on its rescue mission.

While the Harwich men were waiting for their tug to get up enough steam to take them to sea, the Chief Coastguard Officer at Clacton received a telegram informing him that a steamer was aground on the Sunk Sand and a ship on the Long Sand. He passed the message on to the Clacton lifeboat which was launched at almost the same time as the Harwich boat was setting out on its mission to the *Nymphaea*.

By that time, the crew of the *Nymphaea* had, more successfully than *Indian Chief*'s crew, launched her own lifeboats and got the whole crew safely off. They were picked up by a steamer lying at anchor in the West Swim and were eventually landed safely at Gravesend.

But the Harwich men did not know that. They thought it was the crew of the *Indian Chief* that had left their ship, so they made for the *Nymphaea*. When they reached her, at about 3 p.m., they found her abandoned. Understanding at last what had happened, they tried to make for the *Indian Chief* by going round the Sunk Sand Head, but the wind and sea were dead against them and it was getting dark so they went back to Harwich, intending to wait out the night and attempt a rescue again next day.

Meanwhile, battling through a flood tide and heavy seas, it was nearly 7 p.m. by the time the Clacton boat arrived off Sunk Sand Head and it was another hour and a half after that before they sighted *Indian Chief*'s lights half a mile away. It might as well have been much further, for the wreck was on the far side of the Sand and with the wind and sea against them, the lifeboatmen decided not to try to go round the Sand in the deepening darkness. Instead, they anchored for the night to be ready to begin their rescue attempt at first light next day.

Unknown to them, the Ramsgate lifeboat had also joined in the rescue attempt. Unlike the tug at Harwich, the Ramsgate tug, *Vulcan*, kept up steam in bad weather for just such an emergency and within 15 minutes of receiving the message that there was a ship in distress, she had the Ramsgate lifeboat, *Bradford*, under the command of Cox'n Charles Fish, in tow and on its way to the Sand.

A north-east gale was blowing and the seas threatened to overtop the tug at times. It was bitterly cold, too, but the two rescue vessels reached the Kentish Knock lightship and bore towards the Long Sand Head. They could see no sign of the wreck but it was getting dark by the time they reached the sand anyway, so they, too, anchored and prepared to ride out the night and resume their search next day.

During the night, the men in the Clacton lifeboat saw that the light by which they had identified their destination was no longer visible. They waited for some time, hoping it would reappear, but when it did not they weighed anchor at about 3 a.m. and set off to search for the wreck in the darkness. It was a hopeless task with no light to guide them and after a fruitless quest they again had to anchor and settle down to wait for day to dawn.

At daylight, 6th January, they could see they were a couple of miles to leeward of the wreck. Weighing anchor again, they got in as close as they could but, seeing no-one aboard, they turned away and made for the Sunk lightship, to which they reported all hands aboard the *Indian Chief* had been drowned. Then, believing there was nothing more they could do, they turned and went back to Clacton.

In fact they were wrong, although the mistake was understandable in the circumstances. The survivors in the foremast rigging of *Indian Chief* all wore yellow oilskins which provided almost perfect camouflage against the light-coloured timber of the mast to which they were closely bound. They would have been difficult to pick out in perfect conditions. Conditions around the Long Sand that morning were far from perfect.

Luckily, however, the Ramsgate lifeboatmen, after a wretched night, cold and wet despite the meagre shelter of the sail in which they all huddled, saw in the light of the dawn a mast some three miles to their leeward. At once, *Bradford* slipped her towrope, hoisted the mainsail and made for the wreck. The crew knew that if there were any survivors at all they were likely to be in the remaining foremast, although they could see no-one.

Securely lashed into the rigging of *Indian Chief*'s one remaining mast, the exhausted survivors could see the lifeboat. One man managed to let a length of canvas stream away from the mast, a signal to the lifeboatmen who saw it and knew that there were at least some survivors still.

Those survivors, clinging to life after the bitterly cold night, saw the smoke from *Vulcan* and, soon afterwards, saw that the Ramsgate lifeboat was heading directly towards them. Some of them struggled free from their lashings and found rope to which they tied a piece of wood which was floated off to drift towards the approaching lifeboat.

Using the rope, the lifeboat hauled herself alongside the *Indian Chief*, and one by one the survivors were helped into the lifeboat. One man, Howard Fraser, brother of the captain, was too weak to help himself and although he was brought into the boat with the others, he died soon afterwards and was later buried in Ramsgate cemetery.

At about 2.30 that afternoon, the survivors were brought into Ramsgate harbour to a tumultuous welcome by a crowd of about 2,000 people. The lifeboatmen had been at sea continuously for 26 hours. So had *Vulcan*, which was badly battered by the wind-tossed sea.

On 11th February that year, the Duke of Edinburgh (second son of Queen Victoria) presented awards to the crew of the lifeboat. Cox'n Fish was awarded the Gold Medal of the RNLI and there were silver medals for the rest of his crew and for the master of the tug, *Vulcan*, whose engineer, William Harrier, received a Second Service Clasp. There were silver medals for the rest of the tug's crew, too.

Subsequently, each member of the crews of both the *Bradford* and the *Vulcan* received £25 10s and a medal from a public subscription to which there had been contributions from all over the UK and abroad. The medal bore the words: 'Presented for conspicuous gallantry in rescuing eleven lives from the wreck of the *Indian Chief*, Jan 6, 1881, Ramsgate.' On the other side, was a representation of the lifeboat and the tug *Vulcan* nearing the wreck of the *Indian Chief*.

The Board of Trade investigation into the wreck of the *Indian Chief* blamed the pilot for stranding the vessel, judging that he had not shaped a proper course after sighting the Orfordness lights, making due allowance for the set of the tide. The inquiry found no fault with the ship's master or its officers, nor with the crew of the Sunk lightship, whose first duty was to keep the vessel's light burning and to give information to any passing boat or to the shore if it saw any vessel in danger.

However, concern was expressed about the lack of efficient communication between lightship and shore and when it was discovered that the carrier pigeons had taken two days to deliver their message, it was agreed that a scheme for connecting lightships to shore by submarine cable should be investigated. As a result, a scheme was submitted by the Telegraph Construction and Maintenance Co of London, which would enable lightships to give information, day or night, about any wreck.

In fact, the company did lay a line out to the Sunk lightship and maintained it, free of charge, for a year. But at the end of the year another Board of Trade inquiry decided the cable had not justified its cost and it was taken up again.

The Wreck of the *Benvenue*

In November 1891, the south coast of Kent was lashed by a series of vicious gales that did a great deal of damage both ashore and at sea. There were reports of houses and hotels at Folkestone that had windows blown in, chimneys were blown down and crashed through roofs, and roofing tiles were ripped off by the force of the wind. In Folkestone, too, at least one lady achieved immortality of a kind by way of a report in *The Times* that she was overpowered by the wind as she left her house and was hurled against iron railings so violently that her arm was broken. So did the driver of a butcher's cart, of whom it was reported that he was blown off his seat and the cart overturned.

The havoc caused at sea was no less terrible. A great number of vessels of all sizes were wrecked and others were damaged. Among those that were damaged was one of the Ostend–Dover mail steamers, which was blown into the pier at Dover.

But the most tragic victim of that particular storm was the *Benvenue*, a full-rigged ship of just over 2,000 tons, bound from London to Sydney with a general cargo. She was being towed by a London tug when, off the South Foreland, at 6 a.m. on Wednesday, 11th November, 1891, she ran into a ferocious gale that whipped up enormous seas.

Her captain, James Moddrel, decided to try to ride out the storm and he dropped two anchors in an attempt to hold the ship steady into the wind, aided by the tug. But the seas were too heavy and the towing cable parted. The anchors dragged as the ship was driven relentlessly towards the shore. In fact, the anchors did more harm than good because they prevented the ship from being blown completely on to the beach where the crew could have been fairly easily reached and rescued. Instead, she struck bottom in about seven fathoms of water and at once began to settle.

The hapless crew could only take to the rigging, within sight of the beach but, with the seas breaking over ship and shore alike with ponderous fury, they might as well have been a mile away.

The shore was already liberally strewn with wreckage from other vessels and thousands of people had braved the weather to come down on the beach, where there was nothing they could do but watch as the waves began their deadly business of pounding the wrecked ship to pieces. The men on board huddled together in the mizzen top rigging against the bitterly cold spray and the hurricane force wind.

At low water, the hull of the ship was several feet under water and when the tide turned, her lower yards were only about 20 ft above the waves. With the exception of the sails that were furled on the yards, every stitch of canvas had been blown away.

The Sandgate coastguards foresaw the likely fate of the *Benvenue* as she came past under tow and were on standby from four o'clock that morning. After the ship struck, they at once began to try to get a line aboard with their rocket firing apparatus. They tried all day, until the light failed, without success.

At midday, a field artillery party was called in and they used a 12-pounder breech loading field gun to try to succeed where the coastguards and their rocket-launcher had failed. But the field gun was too powerful. Each time the force of the discharge was so great that the line broke and at three o'clock in the afternoon, that attempt was abandoned.

The coastguards tried again with their rockets, but although a

The *Benvenue*, the morning after she was wrecked by a ferocious gale within a few hundred yards of the shore at Sandgate.

line was, at last, fired across the ship and one of the men aboard came from the rigging to haul it in, his efforts and the hopes of the others on board proved to be in vain, when he hauled in not the life-saving line but only the broken-off end of it. The man was in constant danger of being swept away by the waves washing over the ship and it was only with great difficulty and at considerable risk that he was hauled back to his refuge again.

It was quite impossible for a boat to be launched into the huge seas that were breaking on the beach. The Sandgate lifeboat, *Mayer de Rothschild*, had tried and after failing at Sandgate was taken to Hythe to try again from there. But it capsized in the attempt and one of her crew was drowned.

The Dungeness and Littlestone boats were already at sea, going to the assistance of other wrecks. A telegram was sent to Dover for help and a brave attempt was made by the tug *Granville* to tow the Dover boat out. But when they reached Admiralty Pier, they found that even the tug could not face the mountainous seas, and both tug and lifeboat were swept away eastwards, only finally returning to Dover later in the afternoon.

However, another crew was mustered at Dover and the harbourmaster, James Durden, again sent the lifeboatmen out to attempt to rescue the people aboard the *Benvenue*.

By 9.30 p.m. the capsized Sandgate lifeboat had been recovered and righted and manned by a fresh crew made up of fishermen from Folkestone and other places, together with some coastguards. It again attempted to put to sea.

As though reluctant to embark upon such a mission, the lifeboat clung to the beach, for some time resisting all the efforts of the hundreds of volunteers to thrust her into the water. But at last she relented and slid into the surf, to the accompaniment of a huge cheer from the thousands of onlookers that still thronged the shore. It was dark by this time, but the survivors in the rigging of the *Benvenue* heard the shout and said afterwards that they were much encouraged by it.

More than once, as it battled towards the wreck, it seemed that the lifeboat must be overwhelmed by the sea, but each time it survived and pressed on. It took no longer than ten minutes to reach the wreck and at once the hazardous work of taking off the survivors began. The men had, by this time, been in the rigging of their ship for just 16 hours.

The lifeboat was heavily overloaded for the return journey to

Folkestone and some of her crew climbed out of the boat and returned clinging to safety lines on the outside of the vessel, to make room for the *Benvenue* survivors. The efforts of the Dover lifeboatmen were finally rewarded, too, and they arrived alongside the *Benvenue* only just too late to play a part in the rescue of the crew.

Twenty seven survivors were landed amid great jubilation from the crowd, although the rejoicing was somewhat dampened when it was learned that Capt Moddrel and four other members of the crew, including two young apprentices, were drowned.

The next morning, the survivors drew up a memorandum which they all signed, expressing their heartfelt gratitude to their rescuers and thanks for the kind way in which they were treated by the people of Folkestone, especially (they said) at the Queen's Hotel and at the Harbour Restaurant.

In the afternoon, a special service was held in the parish church, to which all the people of the town were summoned by the town crier. There was a large congregation which included all the survivors of the *Benvenue*, who were issued with new clothing by the local secretary of the Shipwrecked Mariners' Society.

The chief mate of the *Benvenue*, Samuel Webster, afterwards told the full story. As they reached the South Foreland that Wednesday morning, the wind had blown very hard from the south-west. At nine o'clock the gale increased to hurricane force and the seas were enormous. By the time they were off Sandgate, the vessel had become quite unmanageable. They decided to drop both anchors but even these, together with the tug, were not enough to hold the ship at sea and she drifted in towards the shore at Seabrook. When they were within a few hundred yards of the beach, at between six and seven o'clock, they heard a heavy crash and knew they had struck bottom.

The *Benvenue* started to sink at once and in less than 15 minutes she had disappeared beneath the waves, with only her masts still above water. No attempt was made to lower the boats, which could not have survived such seas in any case. Instead, everyone aboard was ordered into the rigging.

Mr Webster, meanwhile, hurried below for a rocket so that they could signal for help. On his way up again, he collected the captain, who was helped aloft to safety. Then the mate, too, clambered into the rigging and secured himself as best he could. But the captain almost immediately went down on to the deck again, apparently meaning to go to his cabin to fetch his pipe. Before he could do so, the force of water pouring in below decks forced up the hatches and the sea surged across the deck, washing the captain into his cabin and drowning him there.

The mate said they were able to watch the efforts to launch the lifeboat from the shore, but he personally did not believe, even if the boat had put out, it could have effected a rescue in the sort of conditions that prevailed at that time. He added that, although some of the crew thought there was no real hope of rescue, it was nevertheless of some comfort to them to be able to see the strenuous efforts that were being made on their behalf.

Two of the men who were drowned lost their lives because they came back down from the rigging on to the deck of the sinking ship, intending to jump overboard and swim to the shore. Seeing that such a thing was quite impossible, when they tried to return to the safety of the rigging they were unable to do so because the ship was sinking beneath them. They equipped themselves with lifebelts and entrusted themselves to the sea after all, but were quickly swept away.

One of the apprentices who drowned was a lad of about 14 years of age. It was his first voyage and after the ship struck, someone put a lifebelt around him. He was washed against a rail and his head was badly cut but the second mate, Sidney Belson, managed to grab him and prevent his being washed overboard. A moment later, however, another wave threatened to take both man and boy into the sea and the boy was wrenched from the mate's grasp. Still wearing the lifebelt, he struck out for the shore, but he was carried out to sea and was lost. The other boy was washed off the deck at the moment the ship foundered.

Some of the rockets that were fired from the shore in the attempt to get a ship-to-shore line secured, hit the crewmen and one was quite badly injured in this way. Several of the survivors had rope marks across their faces, made by the flying lines.

On Thursday, all the survivors from the *Benvenue* left Folkestone for their homes, as guest-passengers of the South Eastern Railway, which gave each of them a free travel pass.

Queen Victoria was so impressed when she heard of the rescue of the survivors of the *Benvenue* that she gave permission for her profile to be represented on a special medal that was struck to mark this rescue. The medal was awarded to each crew member of the lifeboat. In addition, Cox'n Hennessy was awarded the Albert Medal Second Class and Second Cox'n Sadler received the silver medal of the RNLI.

The lifeboat crew also received £100 among them all from Miss de Rothschild, who had presented the boat to the town a few years before. It had been her wish that the money should go to the crew that made the first rescue in the *Mayer de Rothschild*.

The Nayland Nine

From 28th November until 2nd December, 1897, Margate was hit by the worst storms in its history, worse even than those of 1953 which destroyed the lighthouse and 1978 when the pier was wrecked.

Cyclonic winds reached gale force and during four days blew at full hurricane force from the north-north-west, leaving the entire Thanet coastline strewn with the wrecks of many small craft torn from their moorings. The wind did not allow the tide to ebb from the harbour, resulting in a tidal surge nine ft above the highest previously recorded level. One large collier brig, complete with cargo, was carried half a mile inland, becoming a total wreck and scattering coal far and wide.

Among the very many victims of this great storm at sea was the ship *Persian Empire*, which went aground on the far side of Margate Sands after she was in collision with a steamship.

The Margate surf boat *Friend of All Nations* and the RNLI lifeboat *Quiver* were both launched into the maelstrom to go to the rescue of the *Persian Empire*. The first craft away was the surf boat, at 5.30 a.m. on 2nd December. It put out to sea with its crew of twelve and Charles Troughton, Superintendent of Margate Ambulance Association. Surf boats were private life-boats that were built to local design and maintained by a civic authority. In the 21 years since it had first come on station at Margate, the *Friend of All Nations* had saved 395 lives in many

The memorial on the Marine Terrace promenade to the crew of *The Friend of All Nations*, who lost their lives in their attempt to rescue the crew of the *Persian Empire*.

daring rescues around the Thanet coast, but her attempt to help the *Persian Empire* was to be her last.

As the boat negotiated the harbour mouth, it was struck by a huge roller, followed almost immediately by another. The first made the boat heel over until its mast and sail were almost horizontal. The second filled the sail with water and the little boat capsized.

The RNLI boat, *Quiver*, was a much more efficient and weatherly craft when it came on station in 1866, a gift of the Quiver Magazine Lifeboat Fund. It was in this boat that the first RNLI Medal was won by a Margate crewman when, in 1871, Cox'n William Grant was awarded the medal for his leadership of the rescue of the crew of six from the brig *Sarah of Sunderland*, which was wrecked on Margate Sands.

While the *Friend of All Nations* was being swept, upside down, on to the Nayland Rock, with four survivors clinging to it, three on the hull and one under it, the *Quiver* continued on her mission of mercy to rescue, successfully, the crew of the *Persian Empire*.

Nine of the men who set out in the surf boat that morning were drowned. At their inquest, the Coroner was told some of the bodies of the drowned men were almost impossible to identify because they had been dragged face down over the jagged rocks of the Nayland before they could be recovered. Most of them had worn seaboots, oilskins and heavy clothing, but none had put on lifejackets, even though they were provided.

The funeral of the nine Margate men was attended by more than a thousand mourners. The deaths aroused the sympathies of the entire nation and a subscription fund was opened for the relief of their five widows and 17 orphans which raised almost £10,000 in a few days. Contributions came from as far away as Australia, America and South Africa. The *Daily Telegraph* alone collected £1,373 from its readers and Queen Victoria sent a donation of £35.

The men were buried together in a communal grave in Margate cemetery which was surmounted by an impressive memorial in white marble, inscribed: 'In Memory of the Nine Heroic Men.' The memorial was designed in the form of a rock surmounted by an anchor, rope and lifebelt and had the figure of Hope kneeling in sorrow beside it. It is still there; one of the most distinctive memorials in the cemetery today.

Another memorial, a life-sized bronze statue of a lifeboatman clad in oilskins and cork lifebelt, standing on a rock with his right hand raised to shield his eyes as he gazes out to sea, was erected on the Marine Terrace promenade overlooking the Nayland Rock. It is a familiar landmark in Margate today, not far from the town's station and information centre. Its sculptor, F. Callcott, RA, based his design for the statue on figures and accoutrements featured on the reverse of the Edward VII Lifeboat Medal.

The *Friend of All Nations* was replaced by another boat of the same name, this time a self-righting boat which served from 1901 to 1940. She was, in fact, the Duty Lifeboat during the Dunkirk evacuation in 1940. Afterwards, she was sold.

Those who lost their lives in the *Friend of All Nations* that tragic morning were Charles Troughton (Superintendent, Margate Ambulance Corps), Cox'n William Philpott Cook Snr, Robert Ernest Cook, William Philpott Cook Jnr, Henry Richard Brockman, Edward Crunden, John Benjamin Dike, William Richard Gill and George Robert Ladd. Saved were John Gilbert, Joseph Epps, Harry Brockman and Robert Ladd.

The names of the drowned men were all inscribed on the memorial in the cemetery, which also bore the inscription: 'This memorial was erected at the expense of the Fund so generously subscribed by the public. It was unveiled in the presence of the committee, the widows and their families, on April 25, 1900 and formally handed over by the Chairman, Mr C F Brown, JP, to the Chairman of the Burial Board, Mr Councillor W H Hughes.'

The gravestone in Margate cemetery of the Nayland Nine. Their funeral was attended by more than a thousand mourners.

The nine men are also commemorated on a memorial slab on the wall in Margate Lifeboat Station. The tablet records that it was erected by the subscriptions of their fellow boatmen and friends in connection with the Missions to Seamen Society, to commemorate their loss.

The Brigantine *Rose*

In the days of sail, every year took its toll of ships rounding the Kent coast, some years more than others. A particularly bad year was 1901 and in the gale that blew up on Thursday, 21st March that year several ships were wrecked – though not all were totally lost – on the Kent coast.

One of them was the 97 ft, 164-ton wooden brigantine, *Rose*. She was scurrying south from Sunderland before a north-easterly gale with a cargo of 300 tons of coal when, with a shuddering impact, she ran hard on to the Red Sands, off the North Kent coast.

The force of the impact split open her hull and within five minutes she had sunk. Her master, Capt George Frend of Whitstable, was in his cabin when the vessel struck. So severe was the damage to his ship that, even before he could leave the cabin, water was coming into it. He pounded up on to the deck, well aware that it was already too late to think about saving the ship. The lives of his crew were his chief concern now.

'Every man for himself!' he shouted as he joined the other five members of the crew in the scramble aloft into the rigging to escape the rising water, already eddying over the deck.

On the mast, the men settled themselves to wait for the arrival of a boat to rescue them. They had just enough time to hoist a distress signal and after the ordeal was over Capt Frend told the *Whitstable Times*, his local newspaper: 'One of the crew picked up a bucket with paraffin in it and some cotton waste. Once in the rigging, we set fire to the paraffin-soaked waste, which burned for about 15 or 20 minutes.

'We were sure the men on the Girdler lightship would see us, as the vessel was not two miles away. But apparently they did not, and we had to hang on until daybreak, having full confidence that when it came help would be at hand.'

In fact, soon after daybreak a warship passed close by the wreck of the *Rose*, but saw no-one and did not stop. Aboard the lightship, the crew saw the wreck, too, but they could see no-one aboard either, and supposed the crew had abandoned ship.

It was not until four o'clock on Thursday afternoon that Capt J. R. Daniels, manager of the Whitstable Shipping Company (which owned the *Rose*) and Lloyd's agent at the port, looked through a powerful telescope and realised that people were still in the rigging of the *Rose*, some of them huddled together and wrapped in a sail for meagre protection against the cold and the wet.

Immediately, he sent a telegram to Margate. Within ten minutes of the telegram's arrival, the Margate lifeboat *Eliza Harriet*, under the command of coxswain Albert Emptage, was launched from the town's pier and put out to try to find the *Rose*. But they had only rough instructions about her whereabouts and it was getting dark by the time they reached the sands. They searched until it was too dark and then turned and made for Whitstable harbour, arriving there at about 9.30 p.m.

The lifeboat crew spent the night at Whitstable and at four o'clock next morning they put to sea again. This time they succeeded in finding and approaching the wreck, 30 hours after the *Rose* had gone aground and sunk.

Sea conditions over the sands were very difficult, however, and it seemed that the lifeboat would not be able to reach the wreck even now. But, by sailing to windward the crew eventually manoeuvred her alongside, using the oars. By this time, only three of the brigantine's crew still survived. The other four had dropped, exhausted and freezing cold, into the sea where they drowned.

64

The survivors were Capt Frend, his Mate Wallace Adams, and seaman John Stevens, all from Whitstable. They were taken off by the lifeboat and brought back, only to find that the tide was too low for them to be landed directly from the lifeboat. They had to be transferred to a dinghy and taken ashore in that.

Capt Frend and Adams were helped to walk to their own homes. Stevens was in a serious condition when he was rescued and he was taken on a stretcher to Rolfe's Harbour Street coffee tavern in Whitstable, where it was quite expected he would die. In fact, though, warmth and care revived him and he, too, survived his ordeal aboard the wreck.

Capt Frend said afterwards that he did not know the names of four of the members of his crew. They all had nick-names, he said, and although they all signed papers when they were engaged, the papers were lost when the ship went down.

One whose name he did know was Darkey Thomas, who was first to fall from the rigging, dropping exhausted into the sea while the rest of them could only watch as he was swept away. Two of the others went mad, first laughing, then despairing and foaming at the mouth. One went overboard at about eight o'clock on Thursday evening and he was followed soon afterwards by the other man. One of them fell from the crossyard and hung by his foot just in front of the others for some time before he finally fell into the sea.

In an interview with a reporter from the *Whitstable Times*, his local paper, Capt Frend said: 'I shall never forget his distorted features, with foam coming from his mouth, as he hung there. How we three who were saved managed to hang on as long as we did, I cannot tell. I kept shouting to the other two to hang on, saying that while there was life there was hope.'

The last member of the crew to fall into the sea was the ship's boy. He had worked in a Canterbury tannery until about two months before. His body was later found impaled on a side-light stanchion of the wreck, on to which he had apparently fallen out of the rigging, only a short time before the lifeboat finally arrived to rescue those that were left.

The incident was described by the *Whitstable Times* as 'one of the most appalling and distressing cases of shipwreck that has ever occurred to our local vessels.' The paper went on to say that great indignation was felt in Whitstable that four people should lose their lives within sight of three coastguard stations.

The paper commented on the captain's statement that paraffin oil and waste was burned for about 20 minutes unseen by the men aboard the Girdler lightship, only two miles away, and it blamed that on lack of observance on the part of the lightship's crew. It hoped a strict inquiry would be made by the proper authority about whether or not a sharp look-out was kept.

Later, it was said that the crew of the Girdler had seen the burning waste and did burn flares and fire rockets to raise the alarm but, presumably, these were not seen from the shore.

There was no official Board of Trade inquiry into the loss of the brigantine *Rose*. Three months after she was lost, a Whitstable coastguard patrolling the beach early one morning found a body near Tankerton Pier. It was thought it might have been one of the crew of the *Rose*, but the body itself could not be identified and the *Rose*'s master and mate both said they did not recognise the clothing as like that worn by any of the missing men.

At the annual meeting of the Whitstable Mutual Maritime Association, which insured the *Rose*, it was reported that during the year ended October 1901 there had been no fewer than 29 shipwrecks, two of which were total losses. The unidentified body could as easily have been that of one of the crews.

Sisters Under The Sands

After the 5,730-ton Brocklebank liner *Mahratta* went aground on a falling tide on the Fork Spit off Deal at 3.15 a.m. on Good Friday, 9th April, 1909, the combined power of nine powerful tugs could not free her from the practised tenacity of the sand. Her shipwreck was part of a sequence of calamitous events that suggested Fate had cast a covetous eye on the *Mahratta* and ordained that her career should end off the Kent coast that Easter weekend, despite all human effort to save her.

It had taken the steamer 34 days to voyage from Calcutta, bound for London and Dundee with a crew of 90, a cargo of tea, rubber, jute and rice, and 17 passengers. All but the jute, which was bound for Dundee, was to be offloaded at London.

After the ship passed Ushant during the afternoon of Wednesday, 7th April, Captain William Ellery remained on the bridge almost continuously until he welcomed aboard Trinity House Pilot Philip Finnis. Then he went below, leaving his second mate, Albert Day, in charge. Day held a Master's Certificate and Capt Ellery felt no qualms about leaving him on the bridge with the pilot.

'Give me a shout when we are west of the North Foreland,' the captain ordered as he went below to take a few hours' rest before returning to the bridge for the last leg of the voyage up the Thames into the Port of London.

The ship was travelling at ten knots as they passed Dungeness and they had to port their helm in order to avoid collision with another vessel coming in the opposite direction. The manoeuvre took them off their course a little, and they shaped a new course to bring them back to where they could take their bearings from sight of the Gull lightship.

Pilot Finnis held a First Class Pilot's Certificate and had worked the coast from Gravesend to Dungeness for the last seven years. When he judged they would reach the lightship at about 3.40 a.m., there was no reason to question that judgement. In fact, though, they made slightly better time than he expected and were in the vicinity of the Gull at 3.15 a.m.

Only six months before, the Gull light had been changed. It now signalled four quick flashes followed by a 20 second gap and then another four quick flashes. It was Second Mate Day who saw the light first, but he did not recognise it because it had been changed since he last saw it. He checked the time by his watch and concluded it was some other light because they were not due at the Gull for another 25 minutes by the pilot's reckoning.

'What's that light, then?' he asked the pilot. Finnis peered into the night.

'Hanged if I know,' he admitted.

He afterwards said he only saw two of the flashes from the group of four in a position he did not expect to see a light at all. He blamed a low-lying mist for his failure to identify it. At the time, though, he held the ship's course, still expecting to sight the Gull light in something less than half an hour's time, and it was not until they were almost abeam of the light vessel that he finally realised just where they were.

He at once ordered the wheel to be put hard astarboard and the engines hard astern, but it was too late. The *Mahratta* shuddered as the sandbank embraced her with relentless strength. It was almost as though the great ship knew she was hard and fast at her final berthing.

The time was now 3.15 a.m. As soon as he recognised the full horror of their situation, Second Mate Day left the bridge and hurried below to call out, not the captain, but the chief engineer, Samuel Gibson. Gibson had last been seen by anyone aboard the steamer when he went to his cabin at 11.30 the night before and Day knew he had to get The Chief down into the engine room where all possible steam was going to be needed for the effort to pull the steamer free.

Day hammered on the door of the chief engineer's cabin. There was no reply. A light shone beneath the door and Day tried the handle. The door opened and he stepped inside, almost tumbling over the body of the chief engineer which lay, naked to the waist, on the floor. His throat was cut and a bloodstained razor lay on a table.

Day turned and, closing the door behind him, hurried off to rouse the captain and to report to him the two-fold calamity that had befallen the ship.

The *Mahratta* had run aground on a particularly dangerous part of the Goodwin Sands, where the surface was very irregular. She had driven herself on to a hog's back of sand, with the tide at half ebb and Capt Ellery knew he might have to wait for the next high tide to float her off again. Local boatmen were quickly on the scene with offers to help refloat the vessel, but Capt Ellery declined their assistance in the hope that his ship would refloat itself when the tide turned.

However, when the tide did turn, the sea ran directly across the sands and drove the *Mahratta*, if anything, more firmly aground. Capt Ellery decided there was no time to be lost. The boatmen, whose local knowledge had kept them waiting patiently nearby, confident they would be needed eventually, repeated their offers of help and the captain at last agreed they should come aboard and help offload the cargo to lighten the ship.

The ship was now fast on the sands and clearly visible from Deal beach. A message was sent to the local police about the body in the chief engineer's cabin and after a brief visit the police authorised the body to be taken ashore. An inquest was arranged for that same evening.

Two of the most powerful local tugs, *Lady Crundall* and *Lady Curzon*, put out from Dover to offer their help and they at once set about trying to free the steamer from the sand on a 'no success, no fee' agreement that promised them £1,000 if they did succeed. However, their combined power was not equal to that of the Sands, which only tightened their grip on the doomed steamer.

Lifeboats from Deal and also from the Thanet ports of Broadstairs and Ramsgate stood by and some of the passengers were taken off and landed at Deal later that Good Friday morning. One lady refused to leave with the others because Customs would not let her bring her dog ashore with her. All available Deal boatmen were welcomed aboard now to help unload the passengers' baggage and then to lend a hand with lightening the ship.

The *Mahratta*'s cargo was valued at between £200,000 and £300,000. The tea she carried was alone worth more than £100,000. A major salvage operation was launched. Other tugs arrived from London and the *Lady Crundall* and *Lady Curzon* were augmented by the tugs *Liberia*, *Arcadia*, *Commonwealth*, *Florida*, *Champion* and *Expert*, which were engaged at a cost of £5,000.

The eight tugs together still could not haul the *Mahratta* back into open water. Even while they tried, the crew and local boatmen were unloading as much of the cargo as they could in an effort to put more water under her. Some of the baled jute and cases of rubber were simply thrown overboard into the sea where the currents could beach them as efficiently and with less effort than the boatmen could.

The *Mahratta* was the biggest ship to be wrecked on the Goodwins for years and the vessel soon became a major tourist attraction. Local boatmen who were not already at work aboard her demonstrated their initiative by offering boat trips out to where she lay so that sightseers could get a closer look at her.

The grounded steamer was taking in water now and the men on board her worked against a background of the constant grinding and snapping noises of steel plates shearing and buckling. Dozens of heavy iron rivets were torn away as the sea scoured the sand beneath her and continually changed the contours that supported her weight.

With about 200 tons of cargo offloaded, the eight tugs, exerting their full power, still could not shift her. On Saturday morning, another tug was added, but the nine tugs together succeeded only in weakening further the already severely strained hull. It was no longer a matter of lightening the ship now, but of admitting that it was unlikely she would ever be refloated and of saving as much of her cargo as possible.

A lighter was sent from Dover to lay alongside the wreck, into which the tea could be discharged, and work continued far into Saturday night. During the night, however, the vessel suddenly broke her back amidships, opening up a five ft wide gap between the two halves. There was confusion and some panic among the men on board her. Some of them jumped into the lighter, which was at once towed back to Dover by the *Lady Crundall*. The rest were taken off by Deal lifeboat and shore boats.

Capt Ellery had gone ashore, but as soon as he learned his ship had broken in two, he returned to her. Engineers who had left the engine room when the water was up to their knees, hurried below again to shut off steam to prevent an explosion and found themselves in water up to their waists. The captain remained on board until everyone else was off. Then he, too, abandoned his broken ship to her fate. By midnight, all the sailors were accommodated in the Sailors' Rest Home. The passengers had already been put on trains and despatched to their intended destination, London.

The inquest on Chief Engineer Samuel Gibson was held on Friday evening and a verdict of suicide while temporarily insane was recorded. His death had nothing to do with the shipwreck

71

and the following Tuesday his body was buried in an unmarked grave in Deal cemetery.

The salvaging of the *Mahratta*'s cargo went on throughout Sunday, but on Monday the wind rose and increased steadily to gale force so that work had to be abandoned. Altogether, 621 cases of tea, 289 bales of jute and 18 cases of rubber were landed at Deal. More arrived on the beaches with subsequent tides.

At high water on Monday, the fore part of the *Mahratta* was awash and the fore hold was full of water. The five ft gap amidships had widened to seven ft and she was listing heavily to port. By this time she had been declared unsalvageable, but further efforts continued to save her cargo as soon as the weather improved again.

Not all of it was, in the legal sense, salvaged. The spirit of the old 'free trade' days was not dead in Deal and coastguards searched some of the local houses. It was a thankless and even a dangerous task. Some of them were quite severely roughed up as they tried to carry out their duty and one actually died after he was physically thrown out of one house. The boatman who threw him out was sent to Canterbury prison to await trial but it was found that the coastguard had, after all, died of natural causes and the man was allowed to return home.

The Board of Trade opened an inquiry at Liverpool, the *Mahratta*'s home port, on 21st May, 1909. The inquiry blamed the pilot, Finnis, whose licence had already been suspended by Trinity House, for not recognising the Gull light vessel and it also suspended the second mate's Master's Certificate for three months because he had not called the captain when he was unable to identify the Gull light. But that ruling caused a public outcry against the injustice of it and in June, Albert Day's Certificate was restored to him.

The captain, Capt Ellery, retired from seagoing and took a Board of Trade job as Examiner for Certificates of Competence for the North East of England.

The *Mahratta* eventually joined that apparently endless roll of fine ships engulfed entirely by the Goodwin Sands. But not before a strange and ironic sequel had made her unique among Goodwins shipwrecks.

Her owners, T. and J. Brocklebank of Liverpool, named a second vessel *Mahratta* and in August 1939 she, too, sailed from Calcutta for London. Before she reached English home waters, however, the country was at war with Germany and the second *Mahratta* joined a convoy of ships for the last leg of her voyage through the English Channel.

But, in the Channel, she broke convoy to pick up a pilot and during the night of 6th October, 1939, she also went aground on the same Fork Spit of the Goodwin Sands that had claimed her namesake just 30 years before.

When she, too, broke up, it was found that she was resting on an earlier wreck and further investigation revealed that the two ships, both with the same name, both owned by the same company, lay side by side. For a time, the two vessels were both visible at some tides but gradually the Sands had their habitual way with the sister-ships and now they lie together, broken and consumed by the most dreaded natural shipping hazard in the world, the Goodwin Sands.

The *Preussen*'s Last Voyage

The German five-masted sailing ship *Preussen* was, at 5,081 tons, the largest sailing ship in existence in 1910. She was built at Geestemunde in 1902 by Hamburg owners and in November 1910 she was on her way from Hamburg to the West Coast of Africa with a general cargo that included about a hundred pianos, several tons of sugar, cement, railway metals and bricks. She had a crew of 48 and two passengers.

There was quite a gale blowing as this handsome vessel came through the English Channel on Saturday, 5th November and off Beachy Head she was involved in a collision with the Brighton Railway Company's mail steamer *Brighton*, which was bound from Newhaven for Dieppe on her regular run.

Both vessels were damaged. The *Brighton*'s forward funnel and mainmast were carried away, her after funnel was twisted and her rail, bar and portside bulwark were all carried away. Her hull was damaged abaft the engine room.

The *Preussen* was quite badly damaged about the bows, too, and her master, Captain Nissen, brought her to anchor off Dungeness. While she was there, the gale worsened and the great sailing ship broke away from her anchorage. She was taken in tow by three tugs, to be towed back up the Channel to where she could put in for essential repairs.

But the Channel had put its mark on the *Preussen* and she was not to escape that easily. As she limped back towards the North Foreland during Saturday night, the towing cables parted and she was driven ashore, midway between St Margaret's Bay and Dover, on Sunday morning. It was a wild night with a strong gale blowing. The wind was full of rain, too. Seeing the sailing ship's plight, the Dover lifeboat went to offer assistance, but was forced back into Dover Harbour by terrific seas that tossed the little craft about like a cork, so violently that her crew had the greatest difficulty in keeping their seats.

The coxswain in charge of the lifeboat reported that the *Preussen* was lying right up against the cliff, her topmasts already gone. He said the lifeboat crew had shouted when they were near enough to the wreck, but got no reply and had not been able to see anyone aboard, although there were lights burning in the deckhouse and other parts of the ship. Several times the lifeboat nearly capsized and in the end she was in such danger herself that she had to be taken into tow by a tug and hauled away. It was only with the greatest difficulty that she was able to return to Dover in safety.

The next rescue attempt was mounted by coastguards, who brought rocket apparatus to fire a line over the ship, so that a breeches buoy might be rigged to bring the crew and passengers ashore. The tide was falling now, threatening to leave the great sailing ship high and dry by low water, and crowds of people gathered on the cliff tops to watch the rescue operation.

The St Margaret's coastguards got their rocket gun into position on the high cliffs above the wreck, but then it was found that it was not going to be possible from there to get a line over the ship. They decided they would have to get the apparatus to the foot of the cliffs before it could be used effectively and, in very hazardous weather conditions and at great personal risk, Coastguard Hughes volunteered to attempt to climb down the cliff on a rope ladder, taking the apparatus with him.

When he was still only part of the way down, a rocket fired by the East Cliff coastguards fell over the *Preussen*'s main rigging, carrying with it a line which at last established ship-to-

The *Preussen*, stranded near Dover. The largest sailing ship in existence at the time, she ended her career on the hazardous Kent coast.

shore communication. Hughes continued his climb and reached the foreshore safely but his risky journey was in vain because when he got there conditions were so bad he could not make any contact with his colleagues at the top of the cliff. It was too dangerous for him to try to return to them by the same rope ladder route he had used for the descent, so he had to make his way nearly a mile along the beach and climb back up to the top of the cliff again by a zig-zag path.

In any case, the crew and passengers aboard the *Preussen* refused to leave her. The ship was lying only about 200 yards from the cliff face, broadside on, and as the falling tide surged about her she could clearly be heard grinding heavily on the rocks beneath, as the force of the gale urged her eastwards to a point where the rocks were very much worse than where she first came ashore.

All through Sunday night and Monday her crew worked to keep down the level of water she was taking in, singing as they did so. But it was a losing battle and by Monday the ship had 20 ft of water in her fore hold. Despite their hopes that they would be able to refloat their ship without help, it became clear that they would not succeed and at about 11 a.m. on Tuesday, there was no longer any room for doubt that the ship was in imminent danger of breaking up. The crew finally admitted defeat and fired distress rockets, requesting help.

A Dover galley in charge of a boatman called Walker put out and took off 18 of the crew and the two passengers. They were transferred to a German tug, *Albatross*, which took them to Dover. A lighter was towed to the wreck by the tug *Lady Vita*, and the rest of *Preussen*'s crew were transferred to that and also brought safely ashore at Dover, where they were taken to the Sailors' Home for rest and recuperation after their three-day ordeal.

Several of the men spoke good English and some had served in British ships. One described how, after the collision on Saturday night, the *Preussen* was making water badly, so the decision was taken to put back to Dungeness and anchor there.

He said: 'We were pumping the whole of Sunday night and the next morning to keep the water down. First our starboard anchor was lost in the terrific gale and then our port anchor went and we were driven out of the Dungeness anchorage. Tugs tried to tow us to Dover but nothing would hold and we were driven ashore.

'The ship struck violently. We have had a terrible time in the gale since she struck and we have been wet to the skin the whole time.

'Capt Nissen is a splendid commander and we all decided to stay with the ship as long as there was any chance of getting her afloat again.

'The men who were working forward had a very narrow escape when the foremast fell. The steel mast with the mass of rigging attached came down practically without any warning at all. It was a miracle anyone in that part of the ship survived.'

The men also described how, on Tuesday morning, the whole crew was mustered on deck by Capt Nissen, who read them a telegram from the German Emperor, Kaiser Wilhelm, which had reached the ship by salvage steamer. In the telegram, the Kaiser expressed his regret at the loss of the *Pruessen* and his high appreciation and admiration for the gallantry shown by the crew in the disaster. When he had finished reading the message, the captain called for three hearty cheers for the emperor, which were given and, indeed, heard by the watchers on the cliff tops.

The *Preussen* broke her back, with the hull broken in two places, on Tuesday. Once all the people on board were landed safely, no further effort was made to tow the vessel clear of the rocks for fear of breaking her in two by the combined pulling power of the several tugs that would have been needed for such a task.

Salvage teams transferred as much of the cargo as possible from the ship to the lighter and an attempt was made to patch her up in order to refloat her on the spring tides in about ten days' time but after she broke up all hope of refloating her had to be abandoned. The largest sailing ship of her time shared the fate of countless smaller vessels that had ended their careers on the deadly hazards of the Kent coast.

A Medway Tragedy

In November 1914 Britain had barely settled down to the idea that the country was at war with Germany, and there were, in any case, confident predictions that it would all be over by Christmas. At sea, the Royal Navy was puffing about its business importantly, never doubting that it was more than a match for any foreign navy and well able to ensure that the country remained inviolate and fed, despite any attempts at a blockade.

One of the safer places for a warship to be, it might have been thought, was anchored in the river Medway. Yet it was there, in the morning of 27th November, 1914, that one of the greatest tragedies ever to befall the Royal Navy wrecked a battleship and killed some 700 of her crew.

The river and the Thames Estuary was a-bustle with vessels of all kinds and all sizes, coming and going and waiting for orders. Among them was HMS *Bulwark*, a 15,000-ton twelve year old warship that had cost more than £1 million to build in 1902. She was a London class vessel armed with four twelve-inch and twelve six-inch guns, as well as a number of smaller artillery pieces and four torpedo tubes. She was capable of more than 18 knots and carried a full complement of between 700 and 800 men.

On the morning of 27th November, HMS *Bulwark* was lying in that part of the river Medway between Sheerness and Chatham known as the Kent Hole, in Saltpan Reach, taking on coal. Overnight shore leave had ended at 7 a.m. so most of her

All that remained of HMS *Bulwark* after the explosion aboard in November 1914. The battleship, armed with four twelve inch and twelve six inch guns, eleven magazines and a full complement of over 700 men had been peacefully at anchor only moments before.

crew were on board, many of them breakfasting below decks although some – the lucky ones – were absent on longer leave.

On deck, the band of the Excellent Gunnery School, which had embarked for duties aboard the vessel, was playing a lively accompaniment to the activities of the rest of the ship's company. The music drifted across the water and was enjoyed as much by people already at work in Sheerness dockyard and at Port Victoria on the opposite bank as by those on board the warship. It was a peaceful sound on a peaceful morning and the war seemed far away and not particularly relevant.

A Royal Marine postman who had gone ashore to fetch the mails for the men on board was on his way back to the ship. It was just about 8 a.m. when he passed a picket boat patrolling the area and as he did so, with appalling suddenness, there was a huge explosion from the *Bulwark*. A tremendous mass of flame belched out of her, followed by dense black, yellow and white smoke which enveloped the whole vessel, veiling her from sight.

On the Isle of Sheppey, people still in their homes felt the shock and heard the rumbling roar. There had been warnings of the possibility of German Zeppelin raids and although few people really believed it would happen, the first thought of many of them was that, after all, it was happening and they were being bombed. But when they realised there was no gunfire, as there would have been from shore batteries if a Zeppelin had been overhead, they knew that this was something even worse than a bombing raid.

Other ships lying in the Medway quite close to the *Bulwark* rocked at their moorings, but there was no tidal surge and no damage was done either to the other ships or to anything on shore. Some people were out and about and when, startled by the suddenness of the explosion, they looked towards where they thought it was, they saw the dense cloud of smoke billowing up from where the *Bulwark* had, a moment before, lain so peacefully at anchor.

Immediately, before the smoke cleared, boats began putting out from both banks of the river and from other ships moored in the river to rescue any survivors there might be. But as the boats thrust through the debris-littered surface of the water, it quickly became apparent that there would be precious few survivors of this catastrophe.

Within one minute of the explosion's ripping out the heart of the warship, she had completely disappeared. All that was left was a scum of debris; much of it, the remains of some of the personal belongings of the 700 or so men who had gone down with her.

The scale of the tragedy numbed the nation, but none more than the people of Sheerness and, later as the news of it spread wider, of the Medway towns and all along the river Medway.

81

HMS *Bulwark* had been built at Devonport in March 1899 and launched in October that year. She was commissioned at Devonport in March 1902 but her home port was Portsmouth and most of her crew came from there, although there were some Chatham men aboard her, too. In any case, the vessel had refitted at Chatham in June 1912 so she was known to the local dockyard workers and before she was recommissioned at Portsmouth in 1912 she had been stationed with The Nore Division at Sheerness. The local people felt she was 'one of theirs' and mourned her loss accordingly.

The death toll was not quite as heavy as it might have been because some of her crew were on leave. Nevertheless, when the roll came to be called, it was found that more than 700 men had died in the incredibly brief minute or two it took the great warship to break in two and plummet to the bottom of the river. Only 15 were saved, and some of them were so terribly maimed and injured in the explosion that they did not long survive rescue.

Exactly what caused the explosion will never be known. An inquiry was held and it was concluded that whatever happened it was inside the ship and not the result of any kind of attack or accident from without.

Rumour, of course, was rife. Some said the explosives stored in the magazine had become unstable and exploded spontaneously. Others guessed some careless crewman had taken an opportunity presented by a moment's relaxation of supervision on the part of a more senior rank to light a cigarette, and had sparked off some loose cordite which had started a chain reaction that ended with the entire magazine erupting.

Another theory was that one of the sailors who were stacking shells in the magazine had dropped one. But since no-one who was in the magazine at the time, nor anyone else who was anywhere near where the explosion occurred, lived to give evidence, there was no way of knowing for sure just what did happen. It was assumed that the explosion began in the after magazine and swept through the entire ship. One eye-witness described a series of fireworks passing from one end of the ship to the other.

Some time later, during the afternoon, when the tide was out, observers reported being able to see where the deck had been forced up by the explosion. But even at low water the vessel was almost completely submerged and it was difficult to be sure of anything. Very little remained above the surface. Her masts and other superstructure had been blown off and sank separately. Some of the bodies were identifiable only by the tattoos on them.

The injured whose lives were saved were taken to the Royal Naval Barracks hospital at Gillingham and it was there that the inquest opened on Saturday. The coroner's jury was made up of 17 men because of the length of time it was expected that the inquest would take. Obviously, there were going to have to be several adjournments and no conclusions could be reached until after the Board of Inquiry had reached its own decision about what had caused the explosion.

The funeral of 21 of the victims was held at Gillingham's Woodlands Cemetery on Monday morning, in drenching rain and half a gale.

One of the few eye-witnesses was Lt Benjamin Carroll, RN, assistant coaling officer at Sheerness. He was on the river at the time of the explosion and was able to describe seeing a spurt of flame abaft the after barbette turret. Then, he said, the whole volume of flame rushed towards the after funnel. He described how the entire interior of the ship was blown into the air and everything seemed to be alight. He was particularly impressed with the way the water remained quite calm and he at once turned his boat back and picked up one or two men.

He was able to tell the inquest that there were eleven magazines in the ship and the force of the explosion was enough to explode all of them. He was asked if he thought a cigarette thrown away could have caused the explosion and he replied that since the twelve-inch charges were in brass cases, he did not think it could.

The War Memorial near Sheerness Docks, commemorating the men of HMS *Bulwark* and the *Princess Irene*, a passenger liner on war service as a minelayer, wrecked in a huge onboard explosion in 1915.

Sgt John Budd of the Royal Marine Light Infantry gave evidence from his hospital bed. He was suffering from a broken leg and burns. He told how, at ten minutes to eight, he was finishing his breakfast on the port side of the second deck when he saw a sudden flash aft. He turned out at once and at the same instant the deck seemed to open and he was hurled into the water. He said he heard no explosion but as he rose to the surface, he saw that the ship had gone. He was picked up by a Service boat.

The Admiralty Court of Inquiry was held under the presidency of Rear Admiral Gaunt. He told the inquest that exhaustive and scientific investigations had taken place and the court was satisfied nothing came alongside *Bulwark* that morning. There was nothing to show the explosion was external and all the evidence, in fact, pointed to its having been inside the vessel.

'There was no evidence of treachery,' he said. 'No evidence, either, of loose cordite and although there may have been loose cartridges in the ammunition passages, I do not think they had any bearing on the explosion.' There were many possible causes, he added, but no reliable evidence. He said many of the theories that had been put forward were untrue and he was entirely satisfied the occurrence was an accident.

Summing up at the inquest, the coroner said it was impossible to discover, because of lack of evidence, exactly how the ignition was caused and the jury returned a verdict of accidental death.

The possibility of sabotage was dismissed with suspicious readiness at the time, although it became a more popular theory of later investigators, especially after four similar disasters occurred aboard Naval vessels.

One of those was the *Princess Irene*, originally a 6,000 ton three-funnel passenger liner but in May 1915 on war service as a minelayer. Some of the conversion work had been carried out on her at Sheerness before she blew up, soon after 11 a.m. on 27th May, 1915 while moored only about a mile from where the remains of *Bulwark* lay on the river bed.

The *Princess Irene* was loaded with mines and her explosion was even greater than that which destroyed *Bulwark*. The loss of life was less. Most of the *Princess Irene*'s crew of 270 officers and men were killed, and so were 77 dockyard workers on board at the time. Very few of their bodies were ever recovered. The only survivor among those actually on board was Stoker David Willis, who was thrown clear by the force of the explosion. He suffered burns, but he lived.

Eyewitnesses told of a vast sheet of flame shooting up with a deafening roar, hundreds of feet into the air. Debris rained down over a wide area. One ten-ton piece of the ship was later found on the Isle of Grain where a nine year old girl, Hilda Johnson, was killed by a piece of iron from the ship which hit her on the head. A 47 year old labourer, George Bradley, died of shock in a field on the Isle of Grain, where he was working.

One man working on a ship more than 1,000 yards away was hit by a piece of flying metal and he died later in hospital. Several other people were injured by flying debris. Charred paper from the vessel was carried by the wind as far as Maidstone, where it littered streets, and windows were broken as far away as Sittingbourne, where several horses bolted in the dust storm that was created in the streets.

The conclusion of the inquiry that was held into the loss of the *Princess Irene* was, again, necessarily inconclusive, although there was strong evidence that the explosion resulted from inexperienced handling of the mines on board.

A Disaster
Waiting to Happen?

American Liberty ships were built in considerable numbers during the Second World War. They were 'kit-built' to an originally British design: comparatively cheap, quickly built, and conceived as expendable. Altogether, almost 3,000 were built and many of them crossed the Atlantic to supply American forces in Britain and, later on, in the rest of Europe, too.

One such vessel was the *Richard Montgomery*. She was the seventh of 82 Liberty ships designed to carry dry cargoes. Built at Jacksonville, Florida, by the St John's River Shipbuilding Co, she was launched on 13th July, 1944 and given the name of an Irish soldier who was born in Dublin in 1738, became an American Congressman and fought against the British in Canada, where he was killed during the assault on Quebec in December, 1775.

The *Richard Montgomery* was a vessel of 7,176 tons, 441 ft long, with a crew of 50, plus about 30 gunners, and after she was loaded at Hog Island, Philadelphia, she was drawing 31 ft of water as she sailed out of the Delaware river into the Atlantic. Having successfully completed her voyage across the ocean, she sailed through the English Channel and into the Thames Estuary, where she was scheduled to wait while a convoy was formed to take men and supplies across to Cherbourg.

The transatlantic voyage could not have been a comfortable one for anyone on board. Even at that stage of the war, there was still an ever present threat of attack from German U-boats, surface warships or aircraft and it would not have taken much to blow the *Richard Montgomery* and all who sailed in her sky high. For, stowed in her holds, were more than 6,000 tons of munitions for the US Air Force.

There were 13,064 general purpose 250 lb bombs; 7,739 semi-armour piercing bombs; 9,022 cases of cluster fragmenting bombs; 1,429 cases of phosphorous bombs; 1,427 cases of 100 lb demolition bombs; 1,522 cases of fuses and 817 cases of small arms ammunition – and more besides. The weight of all this destructive power trimmed the vessel to a draught of 31 ft, three ft more than was usual for a vessel of her kind – and that was important to what happened later.

Arriving in the estuary, she joined a great armada of ships of different nationalities and all sizes, many of which were, like the *Richard Montgomery*, waiting to join the convoy for Cherbourg. She arrived off Southend in August 1944, cleared the submarine boom and her master Capt Wilkie signalled Thames Naval Control Centre aboard HMS *Leigh* (the war-time nom de guerre of the famous Southend Pier) asking for a berth to be allocated to her.

The harbourmaster gave her a place off the north edge of the Sheerness middle sand. His assistant, who was given the duty of telling Capt Wilkie where to anchor, was not very happy about it. He believed the water there was too shallow for a vessel with the exceptional draught of the *Richard Montgomery*, and when his superior officer would not change his mind and allow another vessel with a shallower draught to change places with the Liberty ship, he asked for his orders in writing so that he would not be held responsible.

His forebodings were ignored, however, and the order to berth the American ship was given. The *Richard Montgomery* took up her allotted position and, while her captain, first officer

The wreck of the USS *Richard Montgomery* off Sheerness, as it was in 1978, with over 1,200 tons of explosives remaining in her holds. The wreck still attracts sightseers despite warning signs.

and some of the crew remained on board, the rest of the crew was taken ashore to a hostel for American seamen on the Essex side of the estuary.

During the night of Sunday, 20th August, 1944, some of the other ships noticed that the Liberty ship was swinging towards the Sheerness middle sand. Some of them sounded their sirens to raise the alarm, but the chief officer, who was on watch, did not waken the master and the ship went aground on the sand, where she was held until the next good spring tide, which would not be until about 5th September. Even then, she would have to be relieved of some of her cargo if she was not to break up in the meantime.

As the tide ebbed, the strain on her welded hull increased until some of her plates cracked and buckled with a sound like a loud gunshot. It was heard aboard a motor launch fishing more than a mile away and the fishermen afterwards said they saw the crew abandon ship by lifeboats and rafts. Capt Wilkie was taken to Southend where he was quartered while salvage operations were commenced.

A Rochester master stevedore, T. P. Adams, was called out at three o'clock on Tuesday morning (22nd August) to inspect the cargo and see what could be done to salvage it. His inspection of the vessel revealed that she was not taking in water, so at 10 o'clock the next morning the work of unloading the deadly cargo began, using the *Richard Montgomery*'s own handling gear with winches powered by steam line from a vessel alongside.

The salvage work went on until Monday, 25th September, by which time holds four and five were cleared. During the operation, a force eight gale warning was given and the stevedores on board demanded to be taken ashore at once. During that night, more holds were flooded, the ship dragged her anchor southwards and the stern then separated and moved about 50 ft south of the bow section. There, it lost its buoyancy and settled firmly into the sand.

While unloading went ahead, a Board of Inquiry was held on board. It took from 10 a.m. until 4 p.m. at the end of which time the presiding US Navy Lieutenant Commander found that the master had hazarded his vessel and both he and the chief officer were suspended for twelve months.

The rest of the cargo was abandoned and the USS *Richard Montgomery* became just one more of many wartime wrecks in the Thames Estuary. But she was a bit different from all the others. She was bigger than most of them, for one thing. And the others were not still crammed with such a huge tonnage of high explosives.

While the war continued, it was decided it was safer to leave her where she was, as she was, than to make any more attempts to unload her. Lloyd's Register officially declared her a total loss on 26th February, 1945. When the war was over, it still

Navy divers carrying out a survey of the USS *Richard Montgomery* in 1987. Officially declared safe, despite her volatile cargo, the vessel has been the subject of uneasy debate since the decision in 1945 to abandon her.

seemed the wisest course was to leave her alone. About half her total cargo was removed during the salvage operation in 1944. The other half is still on board.

Today, the still-visible wreck of the *Richard Montgomery* remains where she settled, with the bombs and ammunition remaining in her holds – probably something over 1,200 tons of explosives. The wreck is now in three sections, none sunk very deep into the mud, one and a half miles off Sheerness. Most of the ammunition on board is filled with TNT, which does not deteriorate in water.

Although opinions differ about how likely it is that that little lot will ever explode, and about whether or not the danger becomes more, or less, as time goes by, there is some unanimity about the fact that if it did explode it would be the biggest non-nuclear explosion ever, capable of destroying every building in Sheerness and of washing away the debris with a series of tidal waves that would surge over the Isle of Sheppey and up the Medway to Rochester, Chatham and Gillingham. The explosion would certainly be heard in most of Kent, Essex and London.

91

Nevertheless, despite warning signs and the well-publicised dangers, the vessel has been visited by thousands of adventurous thrill-seekers over the years and fishermen regularly try their luck with the fish that abound in the refuge she affords them.

The question of the danger posed by the *Richard Montgomery* was first raised in the House of Commons in April 1952 when it was again judged safer to leave her where she was than try to move her or her menacing cargo.

She has been the subject of debate, on and off, ever since. In August 1981 she was declared safe by Naval Salvage expert Desmond Bloy after a survey was carried out to assess just how great was the potential danger. Bloy reported that he believed there was no longer any danger of an explosion being set off inadvertently. He declared that even if another ship collided with the wreck in the busy main Medway shipping channel, there was unlikely to be an explosion because, although the TNT might still be effective, the type of fuses used could not last for more than four years in salt water.

Despite further surveys since then, all of which have officially confirmed that assessment, a lurking suspicion persists locally that the *Richard Montgomery* might yet prove to have been an explosive-packed disaster waiting to happen.

It seems there is no way of resolving the argument – except in the one way nobody wants to see it resolved.

Killer Fog

Of all the weather conditions that seamen have to contend with, fog is certainly one of the most hazardous, especially in relatively narrow, crowded passages like the English Channel.

The Channel is notorious for sudden dramatic changes in conditions. Calm can change to choppy, even rough seas, in hours and clear visibility can be reduced to a few yards in minutes.

Modern technology has made it easier to both forecast and to navigate through such changes. In the days of sail, the most common cause of shipwreck was of vessels being blown on to rocks or sandbanks from which there was no escape. The huge amount of power at the command of modern vessels has reduced the number of incidents of that kind but that same power allied to the greatly increased size of some ships, especially tankers and bulk carriers, has resulted in much less manoeuvrability. Today, two big ships on collision course may travel miles before either can respond adequately to commands for avoiding action and collision is more likely than grounding in the English Channel today.

Although collisions in the Channel became fewer throughout the second half of the 20th century, they do still occur, often in the thick fogs that descend on the seaway. When they do, the advances in ship building and design cannot always avert tragedy.

The first half of the 1960s was a bad period for English Channel collisions in fog, sometimes with tragic consequences.

The winter of 1962–63 was one of the coldest of the century and along the North Kent coast the sea was frozen for as far as seven miles out from the shoreline at one time. But, as is so often the case, it was fog that caused most problems for Channel shipping throughout the period.

In March 1961 thick fog was blamed for the collision between the 410 ton British MV *Lizzonia* and the much larger 4,029 ton Swedish ship *Arctic Ocean* in the Dover Strait. The collision locked the two ships together but, luckily, no-one was hurt. The crew of *Lizzonia* were able to step aboard the Swedish ship before their own ship sank.

But it was not always like that. Late on Sunday night, 7th January 1962, the 6,233 ton British steamer *Dorrington Court* was in collision with the Yugoslav ship *Sabac*, 2,811 tons, near the Goodwin Sands, some six miles off the eastern arm of Dover Harbour. There were no casualties among the crew of the British ship, but only five members of the crew of thirty-three aboard *Sabac* survived, including the Master and First Officer.

Sabac sank in five minutes, longer than it took the night train ferry *Hampton*, on her regular cross-Channel service from Dover to Calais, to reach the scene where *Dorrington Court* and other ships in the Strait were already searching for survivors, hampered by the thick fog and by a lot of wreckage strewn across the surface of the sea.

Hampton's master, Captain Norman Dedman, described his involvement in the incident afterwards. He said, 'We were about twenty minutes out of Dover when we received an SOS giving the position of the collision. We altered course and reached the spot about ten minutes later'.

Captain Dedman said he saw only one ship, which seemed to be stopped. He could see winking lights in the water and he ordered boats to be lowered to search for survivors. The men in the boats could hear voices crying out but the fog made it difficult to locate them and Captain Dedman ordered another boat to be lowered to assist with the search. The two boats scoured the area for about half an hour during which time the first of them picked up three survivors and two bodies. The second, however, found only two more bodies.

The survivors were taken aboard the ferry where they received medical attention from two young trainee nurses from Ashford Hospital in Middlesex who happened to be among the passengers.

The Dover lifeboat was launched just after midnight and Dover Harbour Board tug *Diligent* was also despatched to the scene. When they arrived, *Hampton*'s Captain Dedman handed over the search to them and went on his way to Dunkirk, taking one of the survivors and four dead seamen with him.

Two of the survivors and another man who later died were taken aboard the *Dorrington Court* but her anchors had been damaged in the collision and she was too big to enter Dover harbour, so the survivors had to be taken off in order to be landed at Dover, where they were all taken to Dover hospital, suffering from exposure. *Dorrington Court* was able to sail on to London.

Meanwhile, the Dover lifeboat continued to look for more survivors but, after twelve hours, it returned to harbour with five bodies. The crew, led by Coxswain Albert Cadman, believed there might still be survivors out there and they insisted on going out again to carry on with the search, in spite of warnings that a southerly force eight gale was imminent. They were joined at sea by the Walmer lifeboat and together they combed the area for nearly fourteen hours, recovering seven bodies but no more survivors.

Three weeks later, an inquest was held in Dover, where the Coroner recorded verdicts of accidental death of thirteen Yugoslav seamen who died as a result of the sinking of the *Sabac*. Her Master, one of the survivors, was not able to give evidence at the inquest, because he was still in hospital, but the Master of *Dorrington Court*, a thirty-seven-year-old Rugby man, told the inquest that his ship was six and a half miles east-south-east of Dover when he saw *Sabac* on his radar. After the collision, he said, he did not realise the other ship had sunk until he heard voices in the water. He said he picked up two men and one body.

It was only just over two months later that fog was again responsible for a collision in the Channel, although thankfully no lives were lost this time. All thirty-five members of the crew of the Danish cargo ship *Kirsten Skou*, 4,153 tons, were landed at Dover on Thursday, 29th March, by the Dover lifeboat when their ship sank twenty minutes after being in collision with the 4,719 ton German ship *Karpfanger*. This time, though, the crew of the Danish ship were able to take to their boats and were picked up by the German vessel, which transferred them to the Dover lifeboat before sailing on to Hamburg.

Similarly, there were no casualties when the German steamer *Flachsee* became yet another victim of fog in the Channel during the night of Monday, 12th February 1963, as a result of a collision with the 7,151 ton Canadian cargo vessel *Canuk Trader* near the Varne lightship, about nine miles off Folkestone. Visibility on that occasion was reported to be no more than about fifty yards. All the crewmen of the German ship were taken aboard the Canadian vessel and later transferred to the German tug *Seefalke*, which was based at Dover at that time. The Dover lifeboat was launched – it was actually the first call the lifeboat had had for some time – but this time there was no need for a search because all the wreck's crew were accounted for and were brought to Dover without injury.

It was different on 13th June 1963, however, when the 4,240 ton Panamanian steamer *Carmen* was in collision with a Turkish vessel, *Sadikzade*, again in thick fog. *Carmen* was on her way from Takoradi, West Africa, to Burntisland in Scotland with a cargo of bauxite. She was a medium-sized vessel and she was feeling her way through the fog-bound Channel when, eight miles off the South Foreland, just north of Dover, she and *Sadikzade* collided. *Carmen* began to sink at once and her master and most of the crew took to their boats and were picked up by the Turkish

96

steamer. Two men, however, remained unaccounted for and were presumed to have gone down with the ship. Distress calls were broadcast, and Dover and Walmer lifeboats were launched. They were joined by the German lifeboat *Georg Breusing*, which just happened to be on a goodwill visit to Dover at the time. The German lifeboat returned to shore after several hours of searching for the two missing men, but the Dover and Walmer boats remained on station, continuing the search for nearly nine hours before the Dover boat took the twenty-one survivors off *Sadikzade* and landed them at the port.

On that occasion, one ship sent to the bottom was not enough for the midsummer early morning fog, which had not had its fill of mischief for that day. As though to emphasize just how hazardous fog can be to shipping in the world's busiest seaway, almost immediately after *Carmen* was lost, the *Sadikzade* was involved in a second collision, this time with a Greek motor-vessel, *Leandros*, which in her turn then collided with the British tanker *Clyde Sergeant*.

Happily, neither of these other two collisions was as serious as the first, however, and all three ships involved made port successfully without loss of life to any members of the crew.

Less happy, and contrary to the more common experience, however, was the outcome when the 1,056 ton West German freighter, MV *Katharina Kolkmann* was in collision with a little British coaster, 923 ton MV *Gannet*, in fog some five miles south of Folkestone on 29th March 1965. In this David-and-Goliath encounter, it was the larger German ship that came off worse. She was making her way south and west through the Channel from the German Baltic port of Wismar with a cargo of 1,500 tons of pig iron ingots when the collision occurred. Within fifteen minutes, the *Katharina Kolkmann* had sunk, bows first.

Ten members of her crew took to the boats before she disappeared beneath the surface, but four others, including the Master, were swept away. A fifteenth, the ship's cook, was missing and he was presumed to have been trapped below decks and to have gone down with the ship. The four who were swept away were picked up by *Gannet* but the others, in the German ship's boats, drifted in the fog for an hour or so, shouting to attract attention and to help rescuers to locate them. All that time, they could hear ships' sirens on every side and they knew they were at risk of being run down by any one of the vessels they could hear but not see and, more important, which could not see them.

Dover lifeboat put out and was joined by the lifeboat from Dungeness. Together, they searched the area, aided by flares dropped from a helicopter, until they eventually found the ten men in the lifeboat and took them aboard. They were transferred to *Gannet* while the lifeboat continued to search for the missing man for another four hours, without success.

Motor launches were sent out from Dover to rendezvous with *Gannet* and take off the thirteen survivors and ferry them to the port, where they were taken to the British Sailors' Society hostel in Dover's Snargate Street to recover from the experience. Meanwhile, the helicopter plucked the *Katharina Kolkmann*'s Master, fifty-two-year-old Captain Helmut Malinke, from the deck of *Gannet* and flew him to hospital in Dover, suffering from exposure after spending more than an hour in the icy water of the English Channel.

All the time human fallibility continues to make a mockery of so much of the products of human ingenuity, the English Channel is likely to continue to be a dangerous passage for thousands of vessels travelling through it in all weathers and to the crews that are put at risk by that greatest of all peace-time hazards at sea: the potential killer – fog.

Escape – But No Rescue

❧ ◇ ❧

The very word 'shipwreck' conjures up visions of torn sails and broken masts, but shipwreck is by no means a disaster that remained behind in the 19th century or even the early years of the 20th. Shipwreck is very far from uncommon even today and during the two world wars, the Kent coastal waters were scenes of very many shipwrecks of all kinds.

One such we have already noticed: the bomb-ship USS *Richard Montgomery*. The same coast has hosted several war-ship wrecks in peacetime, too. One of the most tragic was the Second World War submarine, HMS *Truculent* (P315) which sank in the Thames Estuary quite close to the Shivering Sands Fort, almost midway between the Isle of Sheppey and Southend, during the night of Thursday, 12th January, 1950.

Truculent was a T-class submarine, originally launched at Barrow. That morning in January, she left the river Medway for routine trials at sea. Aboard, she carried her normal crew of 60 and also a number of skilled workers from Chatham dockyard, so there were 78 men aboard her altogether. The boat was equipped with a number of new items of gear which were to be tested that day. When the tests were completed off the Essex coast, she prepared to return to her temporary base at Sheerness dockyard.

It was after nightfall as *Truculent* made her way, on the surface and without haste, towards the dockyard. Although she carried her proper port and starboard lights, they were not easy to distinguish from another vessel because they were very low above the water, inevitably on such a low-profile vessel.

As she made her way through the choppy water, another vessel was seen in the same vicinity. It was, in fact, the *Divina*, a Swedish cargo ship outward bound from Purfleet which had just left the Thames carrying paraffin and showing the additional red light warning other vessels under way in the Port of London Authority area (although not applicable in the estuary itself) that it carried an inflammable cargo.

The men on *Truculent*'s bridge saw the *Divina* and the extra light, but not being familiar with PLA regulations, they did not know what it meant. The navigation officer had to reach for his manual to try to find out as the other ship steamed towards them. Lieutenant Charles Bowers, in command of *Truculent*, was among those on the bridge. It was his judgement that the other vessel was showing only part of a two red lights signal, indicating she was not under command and, therefore, at anchor. By the time he realised his mistake, it was too late. The two vessels were on collision course, some nine miles off Southend pier. It was 7 p.m.

Bowers ordered immediate full astern and turned to port, while on board *Divina*, which was in the charge of a British pilot, the *Truculent* had not even been sighted until there was only a very short distance between the two. Even then she was not recognised for a submarine and the pilot did not alter course because the larger vessel had the right of way and he did not think there was any danger.

It was not until the very last moment, seconds before a collision was inevitable, that the danger was finally recognised. *Divina* was ordered hard a-starboard but there was not enough time for her to respond to the rudder fully and the two vessels met with a crash.

Truculent was severely damaged. Only one of the men on her bridge had had time to get below before the collision. The rest were swept off into the water as the boat immediately began to settle beneath them into 42 ft of water.

The rest – 73 men in all – were trapped in the damaged submarine. Lt Bowers had ordered the watertight doors to be closed moments before the impact, but there had not been time to carry out the order. Nevertheless, the men were relatively unharmed, although covered in oil and up to their armpits in water. The forward part of the submarine, including the control room, was flooded and the men were all crowded into the aft compartments.

There was no panic. The shipyard men took their lead from the crew who went about well-drilled procedures. The emergency lighting was on and there was enough air to last them four hours. Rescue was only a matter of time, they told themselves. After all, they were less than 50 ft below one of the world's busiest shipping lanes.

Yet it was that very busyness that was their undoing. Perhaps, if the trapped men had chosen to stay where they were and wait for their rescuers to arrive, all would have been well after all. But there was a danger of carbon dioxide poisoning and when they heard the throb of a propeller passing above them, they supposed it was *Divina* waiting to pick up survivors and they decided to use the escape hatch, which would allow each man, one at a time, to make his way to the surface.

There were not enough escape apparatus kits to go round but what there were, were shared out and it was arranged that those that had them would look after those that did not. The escape procedure was successful. One by one the men left the wreck and bobbed up to the surface where they confidently expected to find a whole fleet of rescue vessels waiting to pluck them to safety from the chilling water.

Instead, however, they found themselves in a dark, cold emptiness. The propellers they had heard had been those of an unsuspecting vessel hurrying on its way quite unaware of the wrecked submarine below the surface.

Those that had escape apparatus helped those that did not but, individually and in helpless little groups, they were seized by the ebbing tide and taken gently but relentlessly out into the even colder and emptier North Sea. Fifty seven men drowned or died of exposure.

The men who had been swept off the bridge were picked up after 45 minutes in the sea. One of them was the Navigating Officer, Lieutenant Humphrey Baker, who rescued Sub-Lieutenant L. Frew, who had a broken arm. These two and three others were the first to be picked up, by a Dutch ship called *Almdijk*.

After 45 minutes in the sea none of the men was able to explain clearly to their rescuers what exactly had happened. Although *Almdijk* signalled that she had picked up the men, it was another 30 minutes before the survivors were in a fit condition to tell a coherent story which could be relayed to the shore. Only then, almost two hours after the collision occurred, could a rescue operation be launched.

Meanwhile, *Divina* still supposed she had struck a small fishing vessel or a motor launch. She, too, began to pluck survivors out of the water. She saved ten men and from them began to realise the true extent of the tragedy in which she had been so unwittingly involved.

When the rescue ships arrived on the scene, nearly three hours after the submarine sank, they took up stations across the estuary, their searchlights playing over the choppy water, hoping to pick out the bobbing heads of survivors. A depth charge was dropped to let anyone still aboard *Truculent* know that now was the time to leave the wreck. But it was too late. There was no-one left aboard.

For the next 24 hours Southend lifeboatmen circled the area. At the end of that time, however, they abandoned all hope and the search was called off. The loss of HMS *Truculent* went into Royal Naval records as the worst peace-time disaster of its kind.

It was not until next morning that news of the tragedy reached the Medway Towns. Prayers were said at school assemblies throughout the area that morning, for the lost men and their families. A disaster fund was started by the mayors of

The submarine HMS *Truculent* being raised in 1950. A tragic misconception resulted in the deaths of 57 crew members in what is considered by the Royal Navy to be the worst peace time disaster of its kind.

Chatham, Rochester and Gillingham, and money poured in. The cast of the Chatham Theatre Royal pantomine, *Cinderella*, made collections from audiences and the ponies that pulled Cinderella's coach on the stage were sent out on to the streets between performances to boost street collections. All sorts of events were held by local people, individuals and organisations, in aid of the disaster fund.

The loss of life that terrible night was not entirely in vain. A number of modifications were introduced in an effort to make submarines safer, including the provision of survival suits with inflatable linings and signal lights. At Gosport, a 100 ft high tower was built so that trainee submariners could be taught how to make a free ascent in escaping from a crippled submarine.

The disaster fund eventually proved to be one of the most successful in the area, raising £53,000 for the dependents of the men who lost their lives in the *Truculent* incident. The last payment was made from the fund in October 1970, to a Portsmouth man, the son of one of *Truculent*'s crew, when he reached the age of 21.

At the Admiralty Board investigation that was led by Rear Admiral Cecil Hughes-Hallett, it was decided that *Truculent* was 'most seriously at fault'. In his judgement, Ad Hughes-Hallett said: 'The central fact remains that Lt Bowers turned to port on sighting the lights when sound seamanship and rule of the road dictate he should have held his course, turned to starboard or stopped.

'It was from this initial error that the train of events which led to the collision followed almost inevitably.'

The Admiralty accepted responsibility for the tragedy but ruled that each party should pay its own damages out of court. The Board decided that if the watertight doors on *Truculent* had been closed, she would have settled with her stern above the water, considerably improving the chances of survival for the men trapped aboard her.

It was two months before *Truculent* was raised from her muddy resting place. A memorial service was held for the victims in Rochester Cathedral and three of the Royal Naval men were buried in Gillingham's Woodlands cemetery.

Channel Pile-Up

Throughout the second half of the 20th century, the ever-increasing number of vessels that made the English Channel the world's busiest seaway also made it one of the most dangerous.

During the 1950s and 1960s, as both the number and the size of the vessels using the Channel to reach English and Continental ports increased, seafaring professionals warned that, unless something was done to regulate the traffic flow, a major tragedy was inevitable.

In 1967, international agreement led to the introduction of a 'rule of the road' for Channel shipping. Vessels travelling into the North Sea were advised to keep to the French side, while those travelling south kept to the English side. But it was only a recommendation and not all ships observed the 'rule'.

By 1970, when bigger and bigger tankers were drawing up to 62 ft of water, Trinity House, Channel ferry seamen, pilots and master mariners were all pressing for a reversal of the rule, urging that northbound traffic should keep to the English side and southbound to the French side and it should be made obligatory. They pointed out that since the present one-way system was introduced there had been an average of one accident a month. The system clearly was not working satisfactorily.

The Department of Trade and Industry, however, dismissed their arguments, saying it could be more dangerous to change the direction of the traffic flow now than to leave it as it was. They argued that it would be impossible to get international agreement for a compulsory 'rule of the road' or to police it if it were achieved.

In March 1967 the *Torrey Canyon* fulfilled the worst fears of the Channel coast counties by running aground on the Seven Stones Reef off Lands End, breaking her back and bleeding enough of her cargo of 100,000 tons of oil to pollute more than 100 miles of Cornish beaches. That disaster was still very fresh in the minds of every maritime county in 1971 when three tragedies off Folkestone cost fifty-one lives and unleashed Kent's first – albeit mercifully tentative – taste of what major oil pollution was like.

It was at about 4 am on Monday, 11th January 1971 that the 20,545 ton Panamanian oil tanker *Texaco Caribbean* was in collision with the 12,000 ton Peruvian cargo ship *Paracus* about five miles off Folkestone. The tanker was sliced in two and exploded. The explosion was violent enough to blow out windows in Folkestone and Hythe, 16 miles away, and homes shook over a wide area along the East Kent coast area.

The Panamanian tanker was sailing empty, bound for Trinidad, after off-loading her cargo of petro-chemicals and petrol at Canvey Island, Essex, and at Terneuzen, near Flushing, in Holland. Although her tanks were empty, there would have been residual gas in them and it was this which caused the explosion after she was sliced in two. The bow section sank almost immediately, but the stern section drifted for several hours before it, too, sank.

Paracus suffered damage to her bows, but was towed to safety by a German tug, *Heros*. The tanker's First Engineer, 33-year-old Oscar Balzano, told rescuers that he was just going on duty when he felt a vibration. He said he did not hear the explosion that followed because of the noise of the engines but then the ship began to list. 'People were running about the ship, which had already broken in two,' he said, 'We put the lifeboat into the water and left the ship.'

The explosion threw several of the crew of the *Texaco*

Caribbean into the sea. Twenty-one of her crewmen were picked up by a Norwegian ship, *Bravagos* and another survivor was rescued by a Folkestone trawler, *Viking Warrior*. Other ships and RAF helicopters from Thorney Island in Essex searched throughout the rest of the night and until the following afternoon, when, just before the tanker's stern section sank, the search was called off. Eight men were still missing, including the tanker's Italian master, Franco Giurini.

The rescued men, some wearing nothing but their underwear, were transferred to the Dover lifeboat and brought ashore, where they were taken to Dover hospital by ambulance. Two of them who were suffering from shock and exposure and one with a suspected chest injury were detained, but the rest were released and spent the night in a Dover hotel before being flown home to Italy. The body of the master, Franco Giurini, was washed ashore at Sandwich later in January and divers recovered the body of another sailor from the wreck of the *Texaco Caribbean* some three weeks after the collision.

Almost immediately after the accident, an oil slick eleven miles long and two or three hundred yards wide began to drift towards Folkestone. Luckily, because the *Texaco Caribbean* had already discharged her cargo, the oil that reached Folkestone beaches during the weekend of January 23 and 24, was relatively light engine oil and not the devastatingly damaging crude oil it could so easily have been.

The accident sparked new moves to make the Channel one-way system compulsory instead of recommended. Questions in the House of Commons disclosed that an estimated five per cent of the seven or eight hundred ships a day that passed through the Dover Strait were still ignoring it. Nor was there any compulsion on any vessel to take on a pilot. The Department of Trade and Industry spokesman, Anthony Grant, said it would need international agreement to make it compulsory and that would be very difficult to obtain.

It seemed that *Paracus* had been on the 'wrong' side of the seaway when the collision took place in the main south-bound traffic lane, on the English side, and the potential for many more collisions of the same kind, involving tankers with highly explosive residual gases in their empty tanks, was very great.

But the *Texaco Caribbean* disaster was only the beginning of a chain of events that emphasised the urgent need to tighten control of traffic using the Channel. For barely had the stern section of the tanker slipped below the surface to join the ship's already submerged bow section than, the very next day, the German 2,700 ton steamer *Brandenburg* crossed the site and ripped out her bottom on the sunken wreck with the loss of another 21 lives.

Although the British government promised an inquiry into the loss of the two ships, they were both foreign-owned vessels and the loss of life occurred outside British territorial waters. In the circumstances, a formal investigation by British authorities was not appropriate.

Nevertheless, at an inquiry held in Germany into the loss of the *Brandenburg* the vessel's First Officer, 33-year-old Peter Trelle, said the ship was travelling at full speed before a violent bump stopped her dead and she began to sink at once. He was thought to have been the last man to leave the ship which, he said, sank very quickly – too quickly for her crew to launch lifeboats or to reach their cabins to get life jackets. They simply jumped into the sea. He told the inquiry he had identified seven crew members whose bodies had been recovered.

The sinking of the *Brandenburg* brought the total death toll in this Channel pile-up to 29. Eight men were lost in the collision between the *Texaco Caribbean* and the *Paracus*, and another twenty-one were dead or missing from the *Brandenburg*.

But even that was not the end. During the evening of 27th February, the *Texaco Caribbean* claimed yet another victim when the Greek motor-vessel *Niki*, out of Dunkirk, sank after hitting part of the two wrecks off the Varne shoals, despite a number of warning buoys and two lightships in the area. The little ship was

109

seen to be sinking by the motor tanker *Hebris* which reported also seeing men in the sea. Lifeboats from Dover and Dungeness immediately put out to search for survivors, supported by RAF helicopters and an air-sea rescue Shackleton aircraft, but none was found. Ten bodies were eventually recovered. The *Niki*'s complement of twenty-one had included the wife of the chief engineer.

There seemed to be no reason why this particular accident should have happened. The site of the wrecks of the *Texaco Caribbean* and the *Brandenburg* was well marked and ought to have been avoidable. It looked like just another example of inattentive seamanship in the world's most accident prone seaway. It brought the death toll in the Channel to sixty-four in four and a half months and, although all the collisions had taken place in international waters, the UK government announced it was taking urgent measures to try to make the Channel safer.

But it was not going to be easy. More questions were asked in the House of Commons and again the government spokesman agreed that while a compulsory 'rule of the road' in the Channel was desirable, and he hoped it might be achieved eventually, it would be very difficult to obtain international agreement and very difficult to police. He also repeated that he believed that reversing the existing one-way system could be more dangerous than leaving things as they were.

It was not, by any means, a unanimous view. One-tenth of all accidents at sea throughout the world were occurring in the Western Approaches and the English Channel and, although the voluntary one-way system was being observed by about 95 per cent of all vessels now, there were still too many that were ignoring it.

On 1st March 1971, the owners of the *Brandenburg* presented thirteen local fishermen who helped in the rescue of the eleven survivors with inscribed silver watches and each man also received a book from the Senate at Hamburg to commemorate their part in the rescue.

110

At an inquest held at Folkestone on 10th May into the deaths of crew members of the *Brandenburg* whose bodies had been recovered, the opinion was expressed that there had been a failure to recognise or to interpret correctly navigational signals. Verdicts of accidental death were recorded by Coroner Norman Franks. The inquest heard that the Trinity House vessel *Siren* was moored near the wreckage of the *Texaco Caribbean* to give warning of the hazard, although her master, Commander Adrian Burnell, said it had not been possible to establish exactly the position of the wreckage. *Siren* was displaying three vertical green lights warning ships to pass west of the signal. First Officer Peter Trelle, who was on the bridge of the *Brandenburg* at the time of the accident, and another officer who was with him, both saw the lights but did not recognize them for what they were. Commander Burnell said the *Brandenburg* crossed on the wrong side of the green lights and sailed directly into the danger area.

Although the Channel pile-up, begun by the collision involving the *Texaco Caribbean* and the *Paracus*, did not realize the ever-present fear of major oil pollution of the Kent coastline, that fear was fully justified later that same year when the 15,841 ton Liberian tanker *Panther* ran aground off Deal on Tuesday, 30th March.

She was carrying 25,000 tons of crude oil, en route from the Middle East to the Belgian port of Antwerp, when she crossed into the south-bound lane intending to pick up a North Sea pilot at Dover and ran aground on the Goodwin Sands. Walmer lifeboat put out to offer assistance and six salvage tugs stood by throughout the night. The fear was that *Panther* would suffer the fate of so many victims of the dreaded Sands down the ages and break her back before she could be refloated. If that happened, the inevitable oil pollution of the nearby Kent coastline would almost certainly be catastrophic.

The German tug *Danzig* was first to get a line aboard the tanker and so claimed the right to control the salvage operation but attempts by the tug to refloat the *Panther* were abandoned after a day of abortive efforts, leaving the salvage companies arguing with the pilot and the tanker's owners about the best way to free her.

Confronting the threat of major pollution, the government declared that if *Panther*'s owners did not send another tanker to take off some of the stranded vessel's oil, it would charter a tanker to do the work itself. The salvage company protested that it would be impossible to get another tanker close enough to carry out the task, but nevertheless the 8,800 ton Swedish-owned tanker *Ledaro* was despatched from Antwerp while tugs again tried to move *Panther*, succeeding only in turning her a few degrees.

On Friday, 2nd April, the off-loading operation began and it was the British coastal tanker *Ardrossan* that lightened *Panther*'s load, at the rate of 80 tons an hour. During trans-shipment some oil was spilled, resulting in heavy pollution of three miles of beach between Deal and Kingsdown and, although the Department of Trade and Industry at first declared that it had not come from *Panther*, it was later admitted that 'it was likely' that it had. A 100 yard slick half an inch thick washed ashore at St Margaret's Bay and beaches at Deal had to be cleared of oil with bulldozers and detergent spray. Kent County Council sent a fishing boat out with a crew of firemen to disperse patches of floating oil before they, too, could be washed ashore.

Panther was finally freed by tugs at 7.21 pm on Sunday, 4th April, on the second high tide of the day, after 6,000 tons of her 25,000 ton cargo had been transferred. She was undamaged and, after anchoring near the South Goodwin lightship, where she could be examined by divers, she was able to continue her voyage to Antwerp.

On Tuesday, 6th April, a 25 mile long oil slick two miles wide was reported between Dungeness and Dover and it began to enter Dover Harbour. Whether or not it was a consequence of the *Panther* incident was not conclusively ascertained but it brought renewed fears of major pollution. However, by 15th April, that particular threat to the Kent coast Easter holiday beaches was declared to be over.

In May 1971 a new 'Highway Code' for shipping in the English Channel was published by the Institute of Navigation, on the eve of a four-Power emergency conference in London. In it, the Institute made a series of recommendations that included the gradual introduction of a system of traffic control in the Channel and compulsory pilotage in the Dover Strait for all large vessels, including tankers.

There were also recommendations to captains of all vessels about overtaking and crossing main traffic flows. They were still only recommendations, however, and even today vessels still make their way through the Channel and the Dover Strait without regard to the conventions, even after broadcast warnings from Coastguard stations. Collisions, often involving tankers carrying huge quantities of potentially polluting crude oil, still occur and the possibility – some say the inevitability – of a major incident continues to haunt the Kent coastal authorities.

Unguarded Guardian

The Goodwin Sands have no special respect for their own guardians. Few vessels can know more about the Sands in their many different moods than the lightships that lie at their stations around the sandbanks to warn other vessels of the proximity of the hazards. Yet lightships, too, are liable to be caught off-guard and wrecked on the very sands over which they stand sentinel. As recently as December 1954, the South Goodwins lightship ended up wrecked on the Sands, with the loss of all hands except one.

The South Goodwins was the first Trinity House lightship ever to be wrecked in a gale. She apparently broke from her two huge sea anchors in an 80 m.p.h. gale at about two o'clock in the morning of Saturday, 27th November, 1954.

At any rate, her plight was first noticed by men aboard the East Goodwins lightship, seven miles east of Deal. They could do nothing but watch as huge waves tossed their sister-ship relentlessly towards the Sands. Watch – and radio a distress call to Manston. But the ferocity of the storm forbade even the intrepid air-sea rescue helicopter crews from taking off and going to the rescue before seven o'clock that morning, by which time the lightship was lying on its starboard side on the sands with the seas breaking right over it.

Lifeboats from Dover, Ramsgate and Walmer all put out to try to reach the stricken vessel, and did so, but were unable to approach close enough to render any assistance. Their crews

114

could only sit, some 700 yards away, knowing it would be suicidal to approach any closer in such huge seas which would have dashed them against the wrecked lightship and smashed them like matchwood.

The first aircraft on the scene was an Albatross seaplane of 66 Air Rescue Squadron. The crew flew over the wreck and reported that they could see one of the two ship's boats torn from its davits. They could not see any survivors aboard.

Eventually, a Manston helicopter piloted by a former Korean war hero, fought its way through the still raging gale to hover over the lightship. The pilot manoeuvred his machine down to 25 ft above the vessel and at that level the crew of the helicopter were drenched with flying spray. Even at 100 ft, the helicopter's windscreen was sprayed with salt which made it difficult for the pilot to navigate his craft into position above the lightship.

At first, the helicopter crew, like the crew of the Albatross, could see no sign of life. But, despite the drenching spray which, at that height, smothered them, the pilot brought the helicopter down to 25 ft above the stranded hulk and from there, peering through the spray, they made out the figure of a man clinging to the port rail and waving to them.

The man was, in fact, 22 year old Ministry of Agriculture research scientist Ronald Murton, who was on board for a month to study bird migration. He had wedged himself into a gaping hole in the ship's side to prevent himself from being swept away by the pounding waves. He was one of four men who had been on the bridge of the lightship during the night, keeping a watch on the Foreland and the East Goodwins lightships. Soon after 2 a.m. they realised they were drifting and were getting nearer and nearer to the deadly Sands.

Mr Murton went below to warn other members of the crew and to tell them to put on their lifejackets because nothing could save them from going aground on the Sands. It was as he was coming up the companionway again that the ship heeled over and at once filled with water.

115

The report in the *Kent Messenger* of the South Goodwins Lightship, the first Trinity lightship to be wrecked in a gale.

He managed to get to a hatch and cling on to the outside of it and as he did so, one of the other members of the crew called to him. He reached down, caught hold of an overcoat and pulled the man through the hatch but a huge wave broke over the ship and washed both men into the sea. Mr Murton lost his grip on the other man but he managed to save himself by scrambling up on to the port side of the wreck where he hung on all night, dressed only in his pyjamas and an overcoat in the freezing cold.

During the night, he heard a man calling from the bridge, but the gale made too much noise for him to be able to make out what was being said or to identify who it was. After a time, there was only the howling of the wind and the clamour of the sea for company.

Then, a little after daybreak, he heard someone knocking and he was able to establish that three men were still alive in the crew's quarters; one fairly comfortable but the other two in less good shape. By this time, the Albatross and the helicopter were in the vicinity and Murton told the three men to hold on, that help was at hand.

The helicopter winched Mr Murton to safety and when they learned from what he could tell them that there was little chance of their being able to rescue any of the rest of the men now known to be still alive on board, they returned to Manston with their one survivor, who was taken to the Manston base hospital and later transferred to Ramsgate General Hospital. He was suffering from shock, exposure and bruising but he was, at least, alive.

The local lifeboats were on station as close as they could get to the wrecked lightship from about 2.30 a.m. onwards. Cox'n A. T. Berion of Ramsgate lifeboat said it was one of the worst nights he could remember in 35 years of lifeboat work.

Two hours after dawn the lifeboatmen could still see no sign of life aboard the wreck, but then they saw the helicopter lowering its hoist and, moments later, the one survivor was hauled to safety. From sea level, they would never even have spotted him.

117

The lifeboats were joined by Trinity House tender *Vestal* and her sister ship, *Patricia*, and from Dover the Admiralty salvage vessel *Swin* ploughed through heavy seas to reach the scene. From Chatham, the ocean-going minesweeper *Romola* brought diving equipment and frogmen.

From what Mr Murton had been able to tell them, the rescuers believed there were seven men who might be trapped, alive, below decks and attempts to save them had to be made before the tide rose again. The gale, far from abating, was if anything stronger than ever by this time and the sea was being whipped to a frenzy as it clawed at the defenceless hull of the overturned lightship.

The Albatross seaplane continued to circle the area for six hours. Then it had to return to base to refuel, but within half an hour it was back on the job with a fresh crew. By that time, the lightship was completely submerged and the surface of the sea around it was smudged with several patches of oil.

As the tide dropped on Saturday evening, exposing the battered hulk again, still lying on her starboard side, rescue vessels were still prevented by the rough sea from getting in close. It was not until dawn on Sunday that two Royal Naval frogmen were able to go down into the ship. They tapped on steel bulkheads hoping that the trapped men might have survived in an air pocket, but there was no reply. For an hour and a half they searched every compartment under water that they could reach; seven rescuers seeking seven trapped crewmen.

Chief Officer Claude Parsons of the Trinity House flagship *Patricia* was carried to a spit of sand on the end of a 40 ft rope from the US rescue helicopter. From there, without oxygen or proper equipment and wearing only his heavy seagoing uniform, he dived again and again to explore the ship.

The helicopter touched down on the exposed sand, too, keeping its rotors turning to prevent it from sinking into the soft sand. Even so, by the time Chief Officer Parsons was ready to admit defeat, the crew of the helicopter had to lever its wheels free from the clutching sand with a steel bar and for a time it looked very much as though it, too, would be added to the roll of victims of the Goodwin Sands.

When the tide rose again on Sunday, only the shattered one million candle-power light tower of the South Goodwins light-ship was not completely submerged. It thrust through the still wild seas like a forlorn monument, marking the last resting place of the wrecked guardian of the Sands.

Only one of the drowned crewmen was a Kent man: Sidney Phillpott of Ramsgate. He was 48 years old and unmarried. His job on board had been to tend the lamp. A Royal Navy pensioner, he had served during the war on HMS *Sovereign* and HMS *Ark Royal*. He had been torpedoed and bombed, but survived to be drowned in a gale some three and a half miles from his native shore.

He had served on Trinity House light vessels around the British coast for the last seven years and had returned to duty from shore leave only a week before the tragedy that added the South Goodwins lightship to the unnumbered toll of vessels that have ended their careers as hapless victims of the insatiable Goodwin Sands.

The Big Blow

The English Channel is internationally notorious for its mercurial temperament. It is capable of violent mood changes which, even today when they are less unpredictable than they once were, can still take seafarers by surprise.

History records some truly great storms at sea off the Kent coast. In past centuries, some of them sealed the doom of great numbers of ships of all sizes and even changed the shape of the coast itself.

The 20th century made contributions of its own to the record, but it is only rarely that even the Channel experiences conditions anything like those that howled in from the Western Approaches during the night of 16th October 1987 – still remembered by all who experienced it as the night of the Hurricane.

That year was altogether a pretty extraordinary one, climatically, with torrential rain, blizzards, gale force winds and severe flooding. But nothing prepared the south coast for what hit it during the early hours of that Friday.

What was to be remembered as the most destructive wind of the 20th century sent its heralds into south-west Kent soon after midnight on the 15th. By the early hours of the 16th the full force of the Hurricane was pounding the length and breadth of the county. Memorably, even some meteorologists were taken by surprise and one weather forecaster famously declared that, while the winds would be strong, there was nothing in the nature of a hurricane approaching.

In meteorological terms, winds that blow at 73 mph for 10

minutes at a time are hurricanes. The winds that howled across southern England during the night exceeded that with gusts of well over 80 mph. Some reached 100 mph or more. In a few furious hours, 15 million felled trees, wrecked vehicles of all kinds and the tangled remains of buildings marked its path of destruction across a great swathe of coast and countryside from Weymouth to The Wash. In south-east England, where the storm reached its peak, one in six domestic properties suffered more or less severe damage, entire roofs were ripped off garden sheds, garages and even factory buildings, and many more properties escaped with the loss of roof tiles, chimney pots and television aerials. There were more than a million insurance claims, most of them from domestic householders.

When the time came to estimate the total cost, it was put at well over £1 billion, most of which was not covered by insurance. Car insurance claims alone accounted for about £25 million. Yet, thanks largely to the fact that most people were in their homes, relatively safely in their beds, the loss of human life was counted in tens rather than hundreds. Some people did not even realize what had happened during the night until they woke up in the morning and saw the devastation all around them.

The truly phenomenal feature of the 1987 hurricane was its complete unexpectedness. The Meteorological Office at Bracknell forecast a moderate though deepening depression south of Cape Finisterre and although it was predicted that unusually strong winds would cross the Channel into France and the Netherlands, whether or not they would hit southern England was less certain.

When the rising wind reached gusts of over 40 mph the lowest part of the depression, which until then had looked as though it would vent the fullest extent of its fury on France, suddenly and quite unpredictably veered to include central southern England in its orgy of destruction.

Inland Kent was preoccupied with fears of more flooding, which had already devastated parts of the county and was threatening to cause more distress and damage in the wake of torrential downpours during the previous days.

In the Channel, through the Straits of Dover into the Thames estuary and northwards along the east coast as far as The Wash, vessels of all sizes were caught up in the storm, the like of which was outside the experience of everyone on board. Two crewmen died when a Cypriot bulk container was overwhelmed by the heavy seas and, although some ships were able to run for cover in convenient harbours and havens, many had to ride out the storm in open water. For modern ships, less at the mercy of the wind than the old sailing ships were, it is sometimes the safest thing to do.

Not, however, the most comfortable for anyone aboard. The Sealink ferry *St Christopher* left Calais for Dover with 150 passengers aboard at 3.30 am on Friday, 16th October, in relatively calm conditions. But before she reached Dover

The *Hengist* following her grounding in The Warren, October 1987. (John Hendy, Ferry Publications)

harbour, the 8,000 ton vessel was being tossed like a toy by 40 ft waves. The door to the upper car deck buckled under the assault, allowing water to pour on to the deck where inadequately secured cars and lorries lurched about, smashing into each other, destroying freight and denying access to crew members who tried to make the vehicles secure. By the time the ferry approached Dover, the harbour entrance was inaccessible, partly because of the violence of the storm but also because that same violence had already caused another vessel, *Sumnia*, to capsize. All through that unprecedently violent night, the *St Christopher* lay off Dover waiting for the violence to subside. It was not until 2 pm that afternoon, more than ten hours after she left Calais, that the ferry was finally able to dock and her badly shaken passengers could experience the blessing of stable dry land again.

Further along the Kent coast, *Hengist*, another Sealink ferry, was less fortunate. She was tied up in Folkestone harbour, secured for storm conditions with a skeleton crew aboard, but no passengers. As the fury of the storm increased, she broke free from her moorings. One after another, the ropes parted and although each one was replaced her captain, Sid Bridgewater of Dover, decided that it had become too dangerous to remain in the harbour. He gave the order to start her engines and head her out to the comparative safety of the open sea. But the storm was not to be thwarted that easily. The ship was rocked by huge waves which swamped the ship's engines, causing them to cut out. With no power and no lights, the 15,590 ton ferry and her crew of 24 were tossed about helplessly and before they could get the engines started again the vessel ran aground on the concrete apron at 'The Warren', between Folkestone and Dover, where she remained firmly aground.

It was then about five o'clock in the morning. The stranded vessel had a huge gash in her side. The thought uppermost in the minds of all aboard was of the all-too-recent loss of the Townsend Thoresen cross-Channel ferry *Herald of Free*

Enterprise which had capsized, with great loss of life, in the cold March waters off the Belgian port of Zeebrugge. Was the same thing going to happen to *Hengist* in home waters?

Ropes were hastily laid from one side of the vessel to the other so that if it did capsize the crew would be able to haul themselves to safety. But they proved to be unnecessary. Rescue teams were at the scene within minutes. One rescuer braved the mountainous seas and tried to crawl aboard with a lifeline, but he was beaten back by waves and wind. Eventually, however, all the crew were taken off *Hengist* by breeches buoy, leaving the ferry high – if not dry – where she had beached herself.

Afterwards, Chief Engineer Peter Philpott told pressmen, 'We all thought we were dead when she was rolling. We thought it was another *Herald of Free Enterprise.*'

For nearly a week, engineers pondered the problem of refloating the ferry and eventually they succeeded. She was repaired and returned to her cross-Channel service duties.

Meanwhile, inside Dover harbour, vessels were tossed about like playthings and several were damaged but, for the 1,600 ton British registered bulk carrier *Sumnia*, disaster came as she tried to seek sanctuary there. With her crew of six, she was on her way from London to Shoreham in Sussex, where she was scheduled to pick up a cargo of wheat. She was travelling in ballast and when the storm blew up, she did what storm-caught vessels have done for centuries and dropped anchor off a lee shore, in this case the Dungeness promontory.

But the force of the storm proved too much for her anchors, which dragged and after broadcasting a Mayday call at 5 am she headed for the preferred safety of Dover harbour. Before that safety could be reached, however, the *Sumnia* had to navigate the southern entrance to the harbour, which involved turning broadside on to the wind which was gusting at up to 100 mph. She was hurled against Admiralty Pier and the breakwater and it was clear she could not long survive the battering she was getting from the colossal waves.

A port tug was sent out, to try to tow the stricken vessel away from the maelstrom in which she was being battered to death, but its help was refused. The lifeboat *Rotary Service* went out under the command of acting Coxswain Roy Couzens and succeeded in taking off two of the crew and the tug was able to rescue another man. But then a huge wave – one lifeboatman afterwards reckoned it must have been all of 70 ft high – poured over the stricken *Sumnia* and swept away any hopes of saving the rest of the crew. The ship was hurled on her side and sucked down.

The lifeboat carried on searching for survivors, until Mr Couzens finally decided to turn away and head for the eastern entrance to the harbour, which promised to be safer to negotiate than the western one which had proved so disastrous to the *Sumnia*. That decision was a vital one. As they made for the harbour entrance, one of the lifeboatmen glimpsed a hand clinging to a lifejacket in the water. It proved to belong to 21-year-old deck hand Mike Traynor, who had been blown off the sinking *Sumnia* and swept almost the full length of the harbour. He was hauled into the lifeboat moments before he must have been swept out to sea. They succeeded in reviving him and he was taken to Dover's Buckland Hospital where he recovered.

The lifeboatmen were not prepared to abandon all hope of finding the other *Sumnia* crewmen and they were making ready to put to sea again when Coxswain Couzens realized that a pain in his chest, which he thought was the result of the buffeting he had endured at the wheel of the vessel, was more serious than he had supposed. He, too, was taken to hospital where he was found to have suffered a severe heart attack. However, the rest of the lifeboat crew put out again without him and searched for the other men, but without success. It was not until a day later that the body of the *Sumnia*'s first mate, Ron Horlock, was found where it had been hurled by the waves, on the top of the breakwater. The little coaster's Master, David Birch, a Belfast man, was never found.

Index